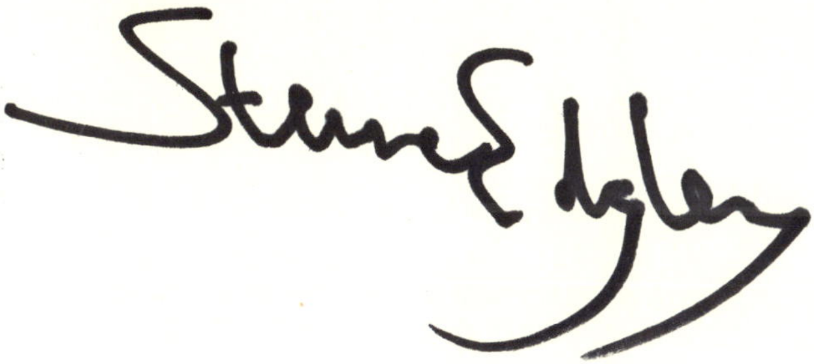

What Others Are Saying about
Dr. Steven Edgley and *Life Between Two Gardens*

"I don't think Steve will survive this," I said to his father as we stood at the foot of his bed where Steve lay unconscious and motionless after a massive stroke. I was never so glad to be wrong. In fact, my good friend, Steve Edgley, not only recovered, but with incredible determination, relearned his speech, regained his ability to walk, and became an honor medical student, resident, and now university professor. He has become an example for hundreds of people in rehabilitation, and he is now advancing the fields for stroke and brain injury recovery."

— Scott J. Kolbaba, MD, *Chicago Magazine* Top Doctor and Author of the Amazon Bestselling book, *Physicians' Untold Stories*

"At some point in our lives, every single one of us must find the honest answers of eternity and our divine worth to our Father in Heaven. Steve has walked with faith and hope through some of life's most difficult paths. His ability to inspire others with his genuine words makes this book a must read. You will feel closer to God and have more hope in your daily life by letting the pages of this book lift you above your own challenges!"

— Chad Lewis, Former NFL All-Pro Player, Author of *Surround Yourself With Greatness*, and Current BYU Associate Athletic Director

"In this book, Dr. Steve Edgley poignantly describes the challenges that occurred when a devastating stroke forever changed his expected trajectory in life. In this memoir, he vividly expresses how his steadfast faith provided him a stable foundation from which to rebuild his life and the strength and insight not only to endure but excel. As someone who was privileged to work with this extraordinary physician, I witnessed how his humbling experience magnified his compassion and empathy for others. This inspiring book highlights the power of personal choices, perseverance, and focused resolve in transforming a tragedy into a blessing, even a gift. For anyone experiencing a heart-rending misfortune in life, it is a touching and stirring message of hope and the power of faith."

— Phillip R. Bryant, DO, Former Division Chief of Physical Medicine and Rehabilitation, University of Utah, Current Division Chief at the Children's Hospital of Philadelphia

"In multiple interactions with Dr. Steve Edgley since his stroke in 2001, I have observed his extraordinary interest and love for others. He dedicates his time and energy to where his heart is, giving fully and freely without hidden agendas. Steve sees everyone, in their own deficiencies, through the eyes of the Savior. Steve continues to choose unwavering faith over anger or disappointment, humbly thanking God for what he is able to do to bless and strengthen others, while at the same time, conquering and enduring physical trials of his own.... The principles on which his life is based—those of goodness, kindness, and generosity of Spirit—define who he is."

— Elder W. Craig Zwick, Emeritus Member of the First Quorum of the Seventy, Church of Jesus Christ of Latter-day Saints and Co-Author of *More to Your Story*

"Steve's story is a remarkable one of faith, family, and courage allowing him to overcome a devastating stroke and become a physician who uses his life lessons to care for others. Having been one of Steve's medical school teachers and honored to assist Steve when he was recovering, I thank God for his life and know this book will inspire many."

— Rev. Myles N. Sheehan, SJ, MD, Current Provincial of the New England Province of the Jesuits and Former Senior Associate Dean at the Stritch School of Medicine of Loyola University of Chicago

"Being mentored by Dr. Edgley is a gift! He has a unique ability to relate to patients and understand the impact their illnesses may have on their lives. As a trainee I am constantly inspired by his optimistic demeanor to overcome any obstacle. He is a man filled with empathy, powered through faith, and motivated by change. Not only change in himself, but finding a way to empower the life of every person he interacts with. I have witnessed firsthand with every new patient that the first words out of his mouth are "I'm sorry." In the medical profession, this is not a common practice, but this speaks to the high caliber of care and empathy Dr. Edgley provides. His book provides insight from a perspective that is unique and invaluable. You'll want to read it!"

— Melissa Kirk, MD, Physical Medicine and Rehabilitation
Chief Resident, 2018-19

"Dr. Edgley helped me through some very difficult times in my recovery from a stroke I sustained in September of 2013. He let me know that there are brighter days through the tunnel of life. He is just one of those 'lead-by-example' individuals. Dr. Edgley was absolutely vital to my recovery. His zest for enjoyment of life is contagious. He is more than a doctor—he is a true friend."

— Brian Hultman, Attorney, Stroke Survivor, and
Ted-X Lecturer, Jackson, Wyoming

"Wow! I could not put this book down. Dr. Edgley's perspective on life's heartaches promotes faith and empowers the reader not only to survive, but to thrive in the face of adversity."

— Dr. Taylor C. Clark, Author of *Beating All Odds*

"I met Dr. Steven Edgley after my glioblastoma surgery for an aggressive brain tumor in September of 2018. During my three-week stay at the University Hospital, Dr. Edgley counseled me often, and provided early rehabilitation, inspiration, and most of all—hope. I have come to love the man and his life-altering work. I trust that anyone who reads this book will find courage and faith to move on."

— Stanford S. Smith, Patient and Attorney

"Dr. Steven Edgley has a unique gift. On a daily basis, he can relate to exactly what his patients are experiencing. Edgley himself suffered stroke at age 28. He quickly changed his career path and is now the Director of the Stroke Rehabilitation Program at the University of Utah."

— Utah Business Editors, "Healthcare Heroes," *Utah Business Magazine*, October 2013

"Dr. Edgley is involved with both clinical aspects of stroke rehabilitation and with research on new techniques and methods to facilitate greater function after stroke. He promotes independence for stroke patients throughout the continuum of care for the goal of providing patients with greater quality of life."

— Loyola University Chicago, Stritch School of Medicine, upon presenting Dr. Edgley with the Early Career Achievement Award in October 2016

"Dr. Edgley has a great understanding of the impact of my stroke and shows empathy for my challenges. He also doesn't condone a "woe is me" attitude. He knows and reminds me that if I want my life to be different, I have to work at it and I will be rewarded. He is absolutely correct and that is what has happened. That is what a doctor should do."

— Anonymous Patient Comment, healthcare.utah.edu, June 2018

"You are forever imprinted on my heart and I will always have gratitude to you for allowing me to come to your very specialized unit where I truly know I got the very, very best stroke rehab care. Just so you know, I am continuing to work my hardest in outpatient therapy—I don't want to waste one moment of the miracle of recovery I have been given."

— Anonymous Patient Comment, January 2017

"*In Life Between Two Gardens*, Dr. Steven Edgley reveals the power that faith can have. After suffering from a stroke, he has used his misfortune as a blessing to serve others, both fellow stroke sufferers and everyone he shares his faith with. This book is a testament that God is always at work in our lives."

— Tyler Tichelaar, PhD and Award-Winning Author
of *When Teddy Came to Town*

"Steve Edgley's story is one of courage, determination, and most of all, faith in the face of all obstacles. Even a stroke could not stop him from creating his own destiny—with a little assistance from God, who had bigger plans for him than he ever could have imagined."

— Patrick Snow, Publishing Coach and International Bestselling
Author of *Creating Your Own Destiny* and *Boy Entrepreneur*

"In *Life Between Two Gardens*, Steven Edgley reveals the power of the human spirit. Faced with a devastating stroke at the beginning of his career, he discovered the truth that his life was solely in God's hands. Today, he uses his experience to help others who suffer from stroke and to bring people closer to God. Every page of this book is truly heartfelt."

— Nicole Gabriel, Author of *Finding Your Inner Truth*
and *Stepping Into Your Becoming*

LIFE BETWEEN TWO GARDENS

Finding Purpose and Embracing Hope Amid Life's Greatest Challenges

STEVEN R. EDGLEY, MD

AVIVA PUBLISHING
New York

Life Between Two Gardens: Finding Purpose and Embracing Hope Amid Life's Greatest Challenges

Published by:
Aviva Publishing
Lake Placid, NY, USA
(515) 523-1320
www.AvivaPubs.com

Steven R. Edgley, MD
801-833-7457
Steve.Edgley@gmail.com
www.LifeBetweenTwoGardens.com

ISBN: 978-1-947937-92-5
Library of Congress Control Number: 2019900971

Editor: Tyler Tichelaar, Superior Book Productions
Cover Design and Interior Book Layout: Nicole Gabriel, Angel Dog Productions
Author Photo: Matthew Clayton

Every attempt has been made to source properly all quotes.

Printed in the United States of America

To Emi, for her enduring support and love.
To my daughters, Ella and Louisa, for their sustaining love.
And to all who struggle in this life, as we all will at times, on our paths between two gardens.

ACKNOWLEDGMENTS

I give my profound thanks to Emi Edgley for permitting me to divert attention to this project and for believing in me, even when that belief represented merely a long-shot, a "surprise comeback." Thanks are also due to Melissa Dalton-Bradford for her mentorship and encouragement from the inception and throughout this writing project; to Michael Glauser and Laurel Day for their guidance and mentorship; to Craig Zwick for his encouragement and vision; to my longstanding friend Taylor Clark for encouragement and guidance.

Thanks for the editing work goes to Stacey Fiala whose dedication of countless hours, especially at the initial phases, made this book possible; to Pat Goodin, Elizabeth Alley, and Michelle Lippold for their invaluable editing and insight; to Pauline Edgley for her encouragement, wisdom, and editing; to Rachel Motschiedler and Melissa Kirk for their encouragement and insights.

My gratitude goes to Patrick Snow for walking me through this publishing process, for coaching me, and for his insightful encouragement. I give thanks to Tyler Tichelaar for his dedicated and professional editing. My gratitude also goes to Nicole Gabriel for the cover design and interior layout.

I give my thanks for encouragement and inspiration to Natalie McCullough who, unbeknownst to her, provided a few profound lines of poetry while I lay mute in my hospital bed; to Matthew Wirthlin for his spiritual and literary advice and guidance; to Richard Edgley for his example of strength, courage, and integrity; to Mark Edgley, Jeremy Rigby, Jon Dalton, Matthew Dalton, Darin Zwick, and Amy Bradford for their encouragement and inspiration; to David Steinberg and Candace Floyd for their encouragement and vision; and finally, to Brian Hultman, Courtenay Marvin, Cynthia Barr, Denis Stoddard, Robyn Mead, Cody Bascom, Kent Anderson, Richard Rogers, and many others for inspiring me.

Think of yourself as dead. You have lived your life.
Now take what's left and live it properly.

— *Marcus Aurelius*

But they that wait upon the Lord shall renew their strength; they shall mount up with wings as eagles; they shall run, and not be weary; and they shall walk, and not faint.

— *Isaiah 40:31*

CONTENTS

INTRODUCTION:

THE FIRE

Imagine for a moment that your house is burning down. The flames are destroying everything in their path. You have just seconds to get out and grab your valuables. In this moment of crisis, what will you take? A family heirloom? A laptop computer or a cellphone? Picture albums? Documents? What precious items will you leave behind? Often in a fire, you don't get a lot of choice regarding what to save.

On a metaphorical level, what would you risk your life to save? What would you leave for the flames, knowing that the blaze would engulf everything in its path? Your talents? Your speech? Your money? Your livelihood? Your physical appearance? Your dignity? If you didn't have those things, would life continue to be worth living? Is your core, your "essence," comprised of something much deeper?

My metaphorical house burnt to the ground on December 7, 2001, when I had a devastating stroke, and nearly everything that was of meaning to me was destroyed. I was twenty-eight years old, a father, a doctor, an athlete, and a Christian. My music was still in me; my race had not yet been run. I thought I was one of the good guys, so I would be safe from such an event. But a stroke, like many tragedies in life, is no respecter of persons, and it literally and figuratively burned everything in its wake. It didn't matter that I was young and fit, that I loved God and lived with integrity. It could have happened to any man or woman. It could have happened to you.

But it happened to me. It struck without warning, like a monster from within just waiting to reveal itself. The demon picked me up gently, only to throw me down and leave me wondering what had become of my former self. All that was left was the shell of a man with a portion of his brain turned to ashes.

An event of this magnitude causes one to reevaluate life's complexities and our most cherished priorities while on earth. In my searching for meaning behind this event, I have, over and over again, come back to the spiritual tenets instilled in me from my youth. In the almost twenty years since my stroke, I have spent much time examining my fundamental values and discovered a tremendous innate value in life itself.

My purpose here is not to evangelize. Nevertheless, I can only express these complex yet sublime concepts in the context of my faith tradition—that of the Church of Jesus Christ of Latter-day Saints (LDS Church). As such, I have gained perspective, insight, and strength from LDS leaders and scripture, which may be unfamiliar to some readers.

After the stroke, I did not have the ability to do everything I had thought gave my life value before, but at the most basic level, I still had the ability to choose my response to what would become painful trials. To achieve meaningful goals, to impact the lives of others, to love—these are the things of infinite value. This realization carried me through those early days and nights immediately after the stroke. Lying still in a hospital bed, I was unable to move, feel, speak, or think in words. To search out and create meaning in my new life became my goal.

Starting over from scratch is not easy for any of us. For me, in the months and even years since my stroke, I have been constantly reminded of the way things used to be. But through it all, I have found that the struggle to *rise* from the ashes the stroke left in its wake has given more meaning to my life. When we overcome the trials and travails of this mortal existence, it transforms our daily and often trite challenges and infuses them with eternal significance. As is the case with most things, improvement comes bit by bit, piece by piece. The challenge for most of us is to have the faith to make the effort for that first step, and then the second step, and then endure to the end. So it was with me, when all seemed to be lost.

I am not under the illusion that challenges and disappointments are unique to me. A large part of the human experience is dealing with pain and suffering. However, within each of us is the ability to find faith, courage, strength, and purpose in our challenges and thereby transform our catastrophic defeats. Through the Lord's grace and goodness, we can fulfill our noblest purposes. I feel as though this knowledge has been a great gift to me. Before my stroke, I thought I knew my purpose. I thought I knew where my life was headed, but almost ironically, through my stroke and rehabilitation experiences, I feel I have been greatly gifted with knowledge of this grace and goodness. This book is my attempt to articulate it as a means to assist you in facing your great challenges in life.

Today, in my role as a physician specializing in Rehabilitation Medicine, I daily come into contact with people who have experienced major, life-changing, catastrophic events. Their responses—both patients and their families—are always unique and special. Some people will have a great prognosis, or potential for recovery, but carry a hopeless outlook. Others will have a bleak prognosis, but will be filled with hope. In each instance, there is much uncertainty and many questions that have no simple answers. Every time I meet new patients, I wonder what their stories will be and how they will deal with the firestorms in their lives—I try to provide gentle nudges to help them see their potential, to suggest there is meaning in the suffering they now feel so they can see love in their lives once again.

As a medical resident on a rotation at the Primary Children's Hospital in Salt Lake City, just three years after my own stroke, I walked into a nine-year-old patient's room where her young mother sat at her bedside. I knew from reading the chart that the patient had experienced a rather severe stroke—a rare event for someone so young. Intellectually, this was an interesting case, but, as usual, not until I met the patient did the fascinating picture of an individual life begin to unfold. I learned she was a bright student, talented pianist, and beloved daughter and sister, and I knew the challenges that lay ahead for her. She would have to fight to regain her former abilities and life-station. Although she and her mother already seemed to know about my similar situation, I recounted some details of my own journey and the path that lay ahead for her. They acknowledged that, as painful as it was, trials bring strength that can happen in no other way.

As I left the room, I told the young girl, "You are very brave." Even though I was confident she would do well, she would likely have lifelong impairments. I also knew I was acting as a mirror, reflecting for good or for bad what she might become. I believe sometimes a person needs a story, an example, someone to give hope, more than anything else, just to stay alive. Stories have tremendous power, and sometimes patients need my story more than my medical care to help alleviate their suffering. I feel a solemn responsibility to share my story when possible.

I feel a tug to express the things most important to me, so I hope others will be able to draw understanding and strength from my insights and experience, for I know struggles are universal to the human experience. Mine is a story of a journey through devastation, a journey to find understanding, hope, and healing by the power of Christ's grace. Perhaps my experience is not at all unique, but speaks to broad and basic truths that apply to each of us, even through hardship and strife.

A specific metaphor gave me comfort in the face of all the loss my stroke caused me at such a vibrant age. The metaphor is: In a forest, the ash and destruction from a fire make way for new growth and new life. Since my fire, my life has been an open meadow with the potential for greater achievement, joy, and love. These fires allow rejuvenation and, more than that, a new start offers opportunities for new triumphs. A stroke isn't easy to overcome, and I anticipate mine will take a whole lifetime, but that's exactly the time I have, in this life between two gardens.

CHAPTER 1

TWO GARDENS

Consider for a moment that the whole of human experience takes place in the finite space between two gardens. All we see and experience is book-ended by the important events that took place in those two gardens—the Garden of Eden and the Garden of Gethsemane.

And so we have this mortal life, filled with trials and travails, but also with joy and happiness.

Think of the biblical account of the Garden of Eden. Envision a place of innocence and tranquility. Everything was provided for Adam and Eve, yet, eventually, this paradise would have to end, like a newborn being thrust out of its mother's womb. Adam and Eve were thrust into a new world, a world we are all born into. But in time, humanity would learn of a different garden, a garden that brings meaning to suffering, where love wins the day. Consider that this is the world we all live in. In my faith tradition, the whole human population is living in this space between two gardens.

In the Garden of Eden, God commanded Adam and Eve not to eat of the fruit of the Tree of Knowledge of Good and Evil. They were also commanded to stay together and bear offspring. Without the knowledge of good and evil, however, Adam and Eve would have been in a perpetual state of innocence and unable to obey God's second commandment to have children. Eve eventually realized this conundrum and the difficult choice they had to make. She made a choice, for God had granted her the power to do so. Eve ate the fruit. It seems Eve did this because she realized humankind would need to experience sorrows and tribulations if they were also to experience pleasure and joy. She had faith that her choice was the correct way forward.

Adam chose to stay with Eve, so he also partook of the fruit, a testament to their mutual trust and love for one another. They were both eventually expelled from that beautiful garden because they had transgressed God's commandment. All seemed to be lost. However, as author Sheri Dew explains in *If Life Were Easy, It Wouldn't Be Hard*, "After being expelled from the Garden, Eve capsulized the mortal experience in this spiritually powerful, single-sentence sermon." She cites LDS scripture when Eve said, "Were it not for our transgression we never should have had seed, and never should have known good and evil, and the joy of our redemption, and the eternal life which God giveth unto all the obedient" (Moses 5:11). Dew clarifies, "In short, during our mortal sojourn we can expect to experience joy and pain and everything in between."[1] And so we have the human condition, this mortal experience, shaped by contrasts: light and dark, pleasure and pain, health and sickness.

Many of us go about our lives oblivious that purpose exists in our sorrow and pain. But sorrow and pain provide valuable paths to growth. We are also often oblivious to our human bodies' and mortal minds' limitations.

I know the concept (which represents a precious belief of mine) of the Garden of Eden and the Garden of Gethsemane that this book is built around is not going to be an easy, or even a comfortable construct to grasp for many readers, probably for multiple reasons. However, if you have faith or even a little imagination, you will see the two gardens concept forms an ideal framework or stage to build upon. On this stage, we live out the mortal scenes of an act that encompasses the portion of our journey that we can remember, with our mortal bodies and minds.

When I was a little boy of maybe six or seven, my brother-in-law, Monte, was earning his commercial pilot's license and would occasionally take me along on his training flights. We would go out in a small and simple two-seat, single-engine plane. It was thrilling, really a miracle, that we were *flying*—something that people, until just over 100 years ago, thought impossible.

Just as seemingly impossible, our own bodies and minds are as miraculous as an airplane. As the "vehicle" of mortality, they allow us to gain experience, and they also allow us to struggle, feel turbulence, experience highs and lows, and see exquisite views from majestic vistas. Although they are marvelous, we know our bodies are mortal and prone to sickness, disease, temptation, and injury. Our minds are similarly remarkable, but they are limited by our mortal capacity of memory, judgment, and emotions. It is no wonder that Book of Mormon prophet King Benjamin described our mortal bodies as "tabernacles of clay" (Mosiah 3:5). Mortality is temporary, so in that temporary mortal state, our bodies exhibit the limitations God intends for this mortal journey. However, one characteristic of clay is its ability to be molded, which offers every human being the opportunity to be shaped, by experience, by choice, by the brain that God endowed us with. The human mind and body do not have a flawed design; rather, the mind and body should be celebrated as the means for growth and to reach our divine potential.

Certainly, when compared to God's immortal body at this time, the differences are stark. As God said in Isaiah 55:9, "My ways are higher than your ways, and my thoughts higher than your thoughts." There are mortal limits to our understanding, and these limits are present for even the most humble and the most genius men and women among us. However, our bodies and minds are part of a divine plan, a plan designed to give us the experiences we need to return safely home to our Heavenly Father. Though we may see through a glass darkly, as Paul wrote in 1 Corinthians 13:12, we can walk by faith through this mortal life. The Spirit helps our minds to develop receptivity to God's love, which, in turn, prompts us and guides us to follow the Savior's example, thereby leading us to peace and happiness, even with our remarkable yet imperfect "vehicles." Indeed, we believe this is one of the conditions we agreed upon in our pre-earth existence. And, since the time of Adam and the Fall, we have been subject to the laws of nature, including tragic injury, illness, and death.

As we navigate our mortal sojourn, we can learn about, and rely on, a different garden, a garden we will not have to pass through, because someone, our Savior, traversed this garden on our behalf.

In the Garden of Gethsemane, the second garden which our lives are bookended by, Christ made up for the shortcomings of all mankind by performing the Atonement, gaining victory over death and sin that we all may enter into His eternal love. Christ showed us a better way to live with His life being the perfect example. He will strengthen us in our trials and help us grow. In Luke 4:18, Jesus quotes a passage from Isaiah that illustrates this point well, "The Spirit of the Lord is upon me, because he hath anointed me to preach the gospel to the poor, he hath sent me to heal the brokenhearted, to preach deliverance to the captives." Luke continues on from the original verse in Isaiah 61:3 by saying, "to appoint unto them that mourn in Zion...to give unto them *beauty for ashes*." Jesus Christ's Atonement is not just for sinners—it is for the downtrodden and the broken-hearted. It can teach us how to rise from and overcome the ashes. The purpose of this life is to ascend, to reach our greatest potential. In this sense, Christ invites us to share in His redemption. Through this we can have peace and hope in our lives, even from the ashes, through our divine Redeemer. Christ can make the events that happened in both gardens, Eden and Gethsemane, meaningful in our times of trial as well as in our everyday lives.

In a very real sense, Christ's effect on our lives "is more than a repairman who reconditions a damaged product. He is an architect who builds the structure originally according to God's primal plan, and then reconditions it even more magnificently after Adam's temporary crash."[2]

In a figurative sense, all humankind is living in this space between these two gardens, even though both events already occurred. This frame, living between two gardens, entails for each of us the veil that was placed over our minds. Through our own human biology, physiology, and psychology, we experience this mortal existence, and the whisperings of the Spirit draw us "home."

In a very literal sense, all humankind is bound by certain conditions that occurred or still occur in these two gardens, and all humankind will be recipients of the blessings that flow from each. The Fall allowed tragedy, misfortune, and calamity to exist in all of our lives, but also pleasure, love, joy, and happiness, especially if we listen to that still, small voice. Disappointments and sorrows sometimes come from wrongdoing, but often stresses and pain come to those who are not to blame—this situation is simply a consequence of the natural world we live in. For this reason, certain elements of this life may seem unfair.

Indeed, certain experiences I have encountered seem unfair. However, we can all have hope in Christ's Atonement, the crucial event in the history of mankind, which started in the second garden, the Garden of Gethsemane. Apostle Jeffrey R. Holland explains, "It [the Atonement] is the sublime reality that sets Christianity apart from all other religions. The message is that a man who was dead did, by his own power, infuse life back into his own body, never again to experience the separation of his spirit from that body in time or eternity. In so doing, he magnificently and magnanimously provided, by that same power, a similar experience for every man, woman, and child who would ever live in this world."[3] This same power is available to each of us before we physically die. This is what is meant by being *alive in Christ*, even here and now.

As I personally fought through the stages of my own recovery from the devastating stroke, which entailed weeks, months, and years of soul-straining effort that continues to this day, I have experienced a parallel experience in mortality of being miraculously brought back to life. And by His grace I have been saved.

Apostle David A. Bednar teaches an instructive process while studying the scriptures. He inserts the words "the enabling and strengthening power of the Atonement of Christ" each time he finds the word grace in the scriptures. Inserting these words as we study allows us to carry-over this concept into our actual lives and actions, thereby allowing each of us to access grace in our lives and gain strength. As Bednar explains, by so doing, in this journey of mortality, we go from "bad to good to better and have our very natures changed."[4] In this way, our trials in life can become our triumphs, through His grace, or the enabling and strengthening power of the Atonement of Christ.

We find an example of this grace in the Book of Mormon with Nephi, who knew and understood the enabling and strengthening power of Christ. When Laman, Nephi, and others traveled back from Jerusalem to the wilderness, Nephi's brothers became angry with him and bound him with cords. Nephi then prayed, not for some heavenly intercession, but merely said, "O Lord, according to my faith which is in thee, wilt thou deliver me from the hands of my brethren; yea, even give me strength that I may burst these bands with which I am bound" (1 Nephi 7:17, emphasis added). David Bednar explains, "It is especially interesting to me that Nephi did not pray to have his circumstances changed. Rather, he prayed for the strength to change his circumstances. And I believe he prayed in this manner precisely because he knew, understood, and had experienced the enabling power of the Atonement."[5]

What seems unfair in this life can become enriching. This is something that I have experienced, as well. By Christ's grace, we are enabled and strengthened, and we can change our circumstances—and rise again, including in this life. Christ taught us how to do this by example, in His mortal ministry, which culminated in the second garden, the Garden of Gethsemane. It is of that sense of the Atonement of Christ's enabling and strengthening power that the Book of Mormon missionary Ammon exclaims, "as to my strength I am weak; therefore I will not boast of myself, but I will boast of my God, for in his strength I can do all things; yea, behold, many mighty miracles we have wrought in this land, for which we will praise his name forever" (Alma 26:12). In the second garden, we are shown how to rise—in this life and the next—through the enabling and strengthening power of the Atonement of Christ.

It's no wonder, as LDS President Russell M. Nelson explains, "We understood this concept while participating in [the premortal existence]. There, as premortal spirit children of God, we were excited to…obtain a body and to experience mortality. When the foundations of the earth were laid, 'when the morning stars sang together…and all the sons of God shouted for joy' (Job 38:4). To be granted physical flesh of one's very own is an exciting and enabling privilege."[6]

Nevertheless, given the mortal limits of our understanding, trying to navigate and make sense of this place is difficult and wrought with challenges. However, we will see on the grand stage of life, though natural laws may have laid the stones to build the set, that we are all unwitting players on that stage. And even though there may be hardship, strife, and evil cast around us, it is love that built this stage—a Father's love—for this stage called earth. "And thus we see the great reason for sorrow, and also of rejoicing—sorrow because of death and destruction among men, and joy because of the light of Christ unto life" (Alma 28:14). We are all players on it, fearsome yet wonderful as it is…this stage, life between two gardens.

CHAPTER 2

PREPARING FOR THE FIRESTORM

In the course of my life, which has been arguably more privileged than most, I have had nearly everything I care about in some way threatened. Perhaps it is a common feature of life to appreciate something only after you realize it could be taken away in a flash, whether it's something physical, spiritual, or, even harder still, related to a cherished relationship. "We don't really know what we believe in or care about until what we believe in or care about is threatened, challenged, or measured," Sheri Dew explains.[1]

I have had many valuable experiences. However, I feel I was unwillingly introduced to a concept Apostle Neal A. Maxwell calls a "compression of events"[2] that would force me to examine the essence of my very being, my ideals, and my belief system. The culmination of these experiences was clearly the stroke that visited me at such a young age. My recovery from that stroke is sending rippling repercussions even today. It is up to me, as it is up to any individual, to turn those ripples into forces for good, rather than forces that tear us and the people we care about down. But, first, let me tell you about one of the best times of my life.

I showed up on the first day of medical school in 1997 with pressed khaki pants, a shirt, and tie, and a smile. It was a warm and humid Chicago morning, and as I walked the short distance from the parking lot to the brand-new medical school building at Loyola University of Chicago, I was already starting to perspire from the heat and my anticipation. I was an idealist and a cautious optimist. I was raised with the idea that whatever became of my life, "if it was to be, it was up to me." However, I also had the notion that "If ye will have faith in me ye shall have power to do whatsoever thing is expedient in me" (Moroni 7:33). At that point in my life, this concept had largely gone by per my plan. I had a sense that the Lord was on my side, but I believed I was the master of my own ship, and God would clear any debris or obstacles out of the way. I certainly lacked the faith to turn over the controls to the Lord. Nevertheless, I felt I had been given a gift—the gift, so I thought, was the compilation of my heritage, upbringing, and talents. My wife, Emi, and I set off on this journey, and I believed the Lord's power would make the way clear for us to steer the ship where we alone determined it should go. I kept this belief gift wrapped tightly, for protection, but I never really examined what was inside the wrapping. I suppose I was like many young, enthusiastic dreamers and idealists, with core principles yet unchallenged and untested.

That first day of medical school, I was excited about the opportunity to begin this new adventure, but I admittedly was feeling a little apprehensive about what it would bring. However, I wanted to feel the enormity of that moment, and I had faith in the future. I was determined to forge forward with as much naïve courage as my twenty-three years would allow.

I thought about what it had taken to get to that school's front steps—the efforts of many people—not just myself—over generations of time. My great-great-grandfather, Joseph Edgley, a stableman to the elite of London, looking for a brighter future for his family, emigrated from England to the United States in the 1880s. Since the Edgleys came to America, every generation has tried to equip its children with tools and resources to improve their stations in life.

My own father was the son of a hard-working, honest man who

owned a small dry-cleaning plant in Preston, Idaho. My father was an ambitious young man, a good athlete, and an untamed leader. As a youth, he earned a meager wage doing back-breaking work on sugar beet farms. When he was eighteen, he secured a summer job in the resort town of Jackson Hole, Wyoming. When the summer work was finished, he loaded his car with his belongings, but, as was the custom, he also took a couple of towels with the Jackson Lake Lodge emblem on them. When he arrived home, he greeted his father, a gentle, loving man. His father saw the towels and gave his son a look of disappointment. My father immediately made the several-hours' journey back to Jackson to return the towels.[3] In my grandfather's household, absolute personal integrity was expected. I believe this work ethic and honesty passed down to me, and in some way, prepared me for the pursuit of medicine. Those two virtues gave me confidence that I could meet medicine's rigorous demands. I felt medicine was an honorable profession I could put my whole heart into.

Years later, my father was forty-four and rapidly advancing in his professional field. As a young vice-president, he was poised to have a bright future as a financial executive within his chosen corporation. He was becoming a financial mastermind and an outstanding leader, and people were beginning to take note. Then he came to the attention of the LDS Church leadership in Salt Lake City. The Church leaders offered him a position in the financial department. At first, he respectfully declined, but upon further prayer and counsel with his wife and family, he faithfully put aside his lifelong career pursuits to follow the path the Lord had chosen for him. He was setting an example for me of turning the controls of his personal ship over to the Lord so the Lord could steer the ship to the location expedient to Him.

As a seven-year-old boy, I was unable to understand the magnitude of the career aspirations my father was willing to let go. Much later, I realized my father's example was one of total fidelity to a higher purpose and of faith in God's direction for our family. It was a lesson in sacrifice for something he believed in. This idea of sacrifice was something my parents and grandparents were trying to instill in me as it had been instilled in every generation of our family.

Although these factors gave me confidence in my medical school endeavor, I could not conceive then that it would also provide a foundation of faith, strength, and fortitude to meet the challenges I would soon face.

In my early years, as the oldest boy in the family, I felt like I was under the microscope. Everyone had high expectations for me. I experienced my first important scholastic competency evaluation in second grade. I did well enough that my parents decided I should skip third grade. I entered fourth grade to sink or swim. It was an awkward time of trying to measure up, but I didn't drown in my new environment. Eventually, I did swim, timidly and cautiously at first, but with time, I was swimming hypothetical laps, and then winning awards for scholastic achievements. I drew strength from this early scholarly experience in medical school and again during my biggest sink-or-swim test after my stroke. These earlier experiences gave me the faith and confidence to act and face whatever came my way. Nothing can be accomplished without action and power, but faith is equally important because first one has to choose to believe they can succeed. D. Todd Christofferson explains, "There is. . . a level of faith that not only governs our behavior but also empowers us to change what it is and to make things happen that otherwise would not happen. I am speaking of faith not only as a principle of action but also as a principle of power."[4] After my stroke, I would have to have faith in action and power; I would have to choose to believe I could succeed.

I eventually ventured out of my childhood shelters. When I was seventeen, I moved out of my parents' home and went to Provo, Utah, to begin studying at Brigham Young University. Then I began to explore and challenge my old adolescent paradigms of the world. Interested in pondering and wrestling with life's difficult questions, I was drawn to the major of psychology and pre-med. This course of study fueled my lifelong interest in the mind and body.

My undergraduate education was interrupted when, like most LDS young men, I chose to commit two years to my church as a missionary. My call was to Tokyo, Japan. I felt peace at being entrusted to learn the difficult Japanese language. At times, it was extremely frustrating, but it was also very rewarding. It was a unique opportunity to look past my own self-interest and devote all of my energy to pursuing a higher cause.

In Japan, I truly converted to the gospel of Jesus Christ. At that time, my testimony was a simple, largely untested, but firm faith in Christ. However, I became enmeshed in the lives of people as we shared both experiences and emotions. I tried to understand others' views and feelings, look beyond myself, and lose myself in the work of helping others. Before returning home, I also realized very few, if any, people would be able to understand and relate to my experiences in Japan—a world away.

About this time, I began to learn a lesson that has served me well throughout my life. I was gaining more confidence, again based on a greater sense of my heritage, upbringing, and developing talents, but I still had some misconceptions about my personal relationship with God and the type of support He gives. In my adolescent view of our relationship, I would decide on my righteous desire and exercise faith that, if I kept the commandments, God would support me in my righteous desires, even to the point of the Lord being "bound" (obligated) to cause us to prosper. Having this incomplete view puts us in a type of contractual agreement with the Lord. I was confident that my desire to serve people by becoming a medical doctor was a righteous desire, so I thought the Lord would clear a path for me.

However, this view of my relationship with God ignored that God sent us all to earth to experience the natural consequences of life here, including love and joy, pain and suffering, and everything in between. We learn and grow through our experiences. My misconception was typical of what many young adults and even some older adults have, especially if they have yet to experience the types of hardship that require reliance on the Savior or His grace to strengthen them.

As a young man, I was still insecure in my inexperienced wings. However, I was learning that confidence and insecurity are two sides of the same coin. In other words, what propels men and women to achieve great things is borne on the back of their sense of confidence and their sense of insecurity. However, what I was lacking was a firm understanding of the Savior's grace—that enabling and strengthening power derived from the Atonement of Christ.

As a young adult, I tried to be faithful to the knowledge I had obtained thus far. I continued my studies and engaged in normal social activities. When I was a junior at Brigham Young University, I was set up with a beautiful girl from the University of Utah named Emi Dalton. I knew right away this girl was down to earth, yet out of this world. I managed to win her heart—a miraculous feat. I think Emi liked my confidence; she chose not to see the insecure side of the coin. She made me better. We were young and in love, so we decided to take a chance and be married.

Our first year of marriage, I struggled through the seemingly endless hoops required for me to get into medical school. Finally, I was accepted to Loyola University Medical School in Chicago. I was thankful someone was giving me a chance because I felt I could become a great doctor, one who could give compassionate service. I gladly accepted the responsibility. Emi had applied to and been accepted to graduate school, but she was willing to forgo it to gain work experience and support our family.

We were excited to move to Chicago to start the next chapter of our lives together. Our six years in Chicago became for us a refiner's fire, filled with the entire spectrum of emotions and experiences. Those six years truly were a "compression of events," forcing us to examine what we truly believed in and cared about. Our experiences during my years in medical school were tempered with pain and trauma, agony, remorse, and loss that drove me to examine and recognize the gifts and talents God had given me. Without those experiences, we may not have recognized, internalized, or received those gifts in our hearts the way we did. We chose, finally, to let the Lord steer our ship, trusting He would guide us in ways of love and support.

Faith and trust are really inseparable. Through them, we can discover the treasure of God's love. And in our case, we discovered that treasure as our faith and trust in God were tested during a time of intense suffering and anguish. However, as the scripture states, the Lord will not leave you comfortless (John 14:18), for we will all experience difficult challenges in this life. A stroke becomes one of those difficult events, with the body torn down to its weakest elements and the mortal brain failing on a grand scale. As such, a stroke becomes a macrocosm of life, for it is a rare event that causes one to completely lose his life, and then be able to work to build it back up. The physical and psychological discord of such an event is overpowering. Trust in the Lord's ability to steer your ship to safe passage is required. His divine ability awaits us and can sustain every one of us in times of prosperity and times of trials. It can be more precious than gold.

CHAPTER 3

SILENT BEFORE GOD

It happened on a Friday, December 7, 2001. I had just graduated from Loyola Medical School, and Emi was busy enjoying raising our baby, Ella. We had chosen to stay in Chicago for one more year while I did my internship training. One unseasonably warm but otherwise routine day in early December, while getting ready for work, quite suddenly the power to speak and move on one side of my body completely left me.

I lay down on the bed on my back. When Emi asked if something was wrong, I tried to speak, but no words came out of my mouth. I tried again. My thoughts were present, but I was losing control of my tongue and lips. Again, I tried, this time more forcefully. A strange, gurgling sound came from deep inside my throat. My heart began racing. It was like a nightmare where you want to scream, but your voice has gone mute. Something as basic as voice and speech was being stripped from me. I tried to sit up, but by then, my entire right side was limp and numb; I didn't have the strength. I was being defeated by some bizarre, internal force. I had no power. Confused by the inexplicable and sudden symptoms coming over me, like nothing I had experienced before, I was unprepared, powerless, and afraid—was this what it felt like to die?

Emi quickly realized, in a moment of pure inspiration, what was going on, and called 911. I, on the other hand, had the strong urge not to jump to conclusions, to wait a few moments, and to figure things out as I had been medically trained to do. However, thankfully, the wheels were already rolling in Emi's mind; I heard Emi say, in a firm, though pressured voice, to the emergency dispatcher, "My husband is twenty-eight years old, and he's having a stroke."

I was realizing that any effort to get up or move was futile. I listened to one side of the conversation between my wife and the emergency response operator.

"Yes, he seems to be breathing."

"Just a minute, let me check." Emi felt my neck for a pulse.

"Steve, can you lift your arm?" I didn't know how to respond. I knew she was asking me a question, but I didn't know what to do with the information. I couldn't lift my arm, but I was not capable of saying, "No, I can't." I was also not able to think to shake my head. Instead, I just lay there, feeling brainless; somehow, my brain had become disconnected from my mouth and my right side.

In a few minutes, a policeman barged into the bedroom. A couple of minutes later, more people arrived and the whole room was filled with a flurry of activity. Paramedics were asking me questions for which I had no response. A penlight was shined into my eyes. Paramedics were tapping for reflexes. Someone was calling out for the stretcher. On the stretcher, I was wheeled out the front door. The warm rays of sunshine surprised me—would this be the final time I would feel the sun on my face? Or was it a gentle reminder that my life is not my own, and that a loving Heavenly Father is watching over me? Either way, that sunshine was a very brief but loving reprieve from the critical situation I was in.

I was loaded into the ambulance and rushed to the local ER in a semi-conscious state. In the ambulance, I overheard talk of a massive stroke. It sunk in at that moment. What I had perceived throughout my medical training as the worst thing that could happen to a person was, in fact, at that very moment, happening to me. My fear and internal agitation boiled over. Waves of nausea came over me as the psychological stress of the situation hit me. Was this worse than death? I vomited profusely in the ambulance, which caused the ambulance to stop, and made my internal agitation and fear even greater—I knew my one and only chance was getting to the ER and receiving an invaluable clot-busting medication. I knew time was of the essence in stroke care: time is literally brain loss.

Soon after arriving in the ER, Emi was told my symptoms were strongly suggestive of a stroke caused by a blood clot in a brain artery. It was decided to give me tPA, a clot-busting drug shown to help resolve strokes when administered early after the onset of symptoms. I knew from my medical training that about 20 percent of stroke patients have immediate resolution of their symptoms after tPA is administered. I knew I was still within the three-hour window from stroke symptom onset when tPA was still an option; past that point, irreversible damage has already occurred and the risks of giving tPA are too great. I knew giving tPA was the most important thing in acute stroke management. But, in the crisis state I was in, lapsing in and out of consciousness, all my medical knowledge was useless. I was at the mercy of my body's physical limitations and the decisions of those around me. Emi made the right decision for me—the nurse hung the IV bag that contained the tPA and we all waited.

Although I wasn't aware of it at the time, for most people, tPA's benefits are best seen a few months after the stroke. A lot of disappointment ensued as the minutes passed and turned into a couple of hours, and still we saw no improvement. At one point, a well-intentioned nurse in the ER said to me, "I'm just going to set these intubation supplies on your bed (he placed them across my chest), just in case—we don't want you to become agitated or try to get up, or anything." That was my cue just to be still and relax, not to become animated, and not even to try to sit up, with no means of communication—like a 6'5" hemiplegic gorilla. The threat of being intubated and sedated, possibly for a few days, was very real in my mind.

When a nurse said, "Now, we're going to move on upstairs to the ICU," I was in the depths of despair and disappointment. Being admitted to the ICU, in my mind, meant the tPA hadn't worked. It meant I wasn't going to sleep in my own bed that night. It meant that this nightmare would continue. . .and all I could do was wait.

My memories are spotty, at best, of those first twenty-four hours. Emi and I were both anxiously waiting for a member of our church, a bishop we knew worked at that hospital, to come give me a special blessing of healing. This bishop was tied up in the operating room all afternoon and evening. Emi asked for an announcement on the hospital PA system, and luckily a stranger, who was a member of our church, arrived without delay.

This kind man came into my room and pronounced on my head the first of three blessings I would receive that night. All three blessed me with a "full recovery." This begs the question, a question I have grappled with over the years, and finally received reconciliation for in my mind, of, "What does a full recovery mean and look like?" I have devoted space to discussion of this question later in this book.

Eventually, after a few hours, I found myself alone. Emi had gone to retrieve our infant daughter, Ella, and no doubt cradled her, both mother and baby receiving comfort, as Emi tried to wrap her head around what had just happened and its implications for our young family.

As I lapsed into and out of wakefulness and alertness, I remember visitors swimming in and out of my field of vision. My two cousins who lived in Chicago arrived and tried to ask me my middle name so they could give me a second blessing of healing. I was awake and alert, but I had no way, even by nodding or shaking my head, of answering this simple question. Later in the evening, my parents arrived from Salt Lake City. I felt ashamed to have my mom see me in this state—mother, "behold thy son," I thought. That first night, my father stayed by my side, keeping watch in the ICU.

In the immediate days after, I would to try in vain to figure out what had happened to my body and to my life. Though I was conscious, I had absolutely no physical control over any aspect of my present situation. Spiritually, I even wondered, *Where is God in my time of greatest need?* I felt no physical pain, but there was a silent intensity to my suffering.

It was like a flash fire in my brain had instantly destroyed all that I had been working for. I couldn't utter a single word; I couldn't write; I could barely move.

I had a long time to think in silence, the first five days in an ICU bed, then on the medicine floor for another week. I was surrounded by people but very detached from the outside world because of the massive communication barrier. After a few days, I still had no way to communicate other than nodding and shaking my head. I had no idea whether it would be this way for the rest of my life. Imagine being left out of every conversation, even when people are talking directly to you. I imagined that situation, day after day, for an entire lifetime.

My mind was full of confusion—confusion directed toward not knowing the next steps to get out of this situation. My medical career seemed like it was over. I had worked so very hard, only to come up short at the final buzzer. I had been going to take care of people—heal people. Now I was the one needing care. And not the usual, brief care needed for a person to get back on their feet after a broken bone or a week of the flu. I was facing the possibility of needing lifelong care. Who would provide this care? My wife? My aging parents? In-home nurses and doctors? This was my reality.

During these weeks of silence, two dear friends who were Catholic Jesuit priests from Loyola Medical School came to visit me. They explained to me that, in their tradition, sometimes they took a vow of silence.

Ignatius of Loyola, founder of the Society of Jesus, whose members are called Jesuits, was a sixteenth-century Spanish knight who was gravely injured in battle. After his prolonged recovery, he "took himself to the university," believing he must first conquer himself, conquer his own mind, before trying to influence others.[1] The vow of silence is an important component of the Society of Jesus.

These Jesuits, my friends, were not obscure people in a far-off land; they were people I had come to love and respect. They didn't explain why they occasionally took this vow; they only explained that its purpose is not to deny yourself from talking; it's to be "silent before God." To listen for what God is trying to tell you. So, I did. Unable to communicate with those around me, I vowed within myself to listen and turn my imposed silence into something better. I vowed to be silent before God. This Jesuit tradition helped me accept my current situation and learn that some people actually choose this way of life.

During my undergraduate studies in psychology, I had been introduced to the Kübler-Ross model, otherwise known as the five stages of grief. This model postulates that people experience a progression of emotional states after a severe loss, such as the loss of a loved one or a terminal diagnosis. At that time, I was going through an incredible loss. Knowing I needed to pass through these five stages became a critical element in being able to move past the hurt and disappointment I was feeling and move on with my life. Kübler-Ross described these stages as denial, anger, bargaining, depression, and acceptance. I experienced all five. My Jesuit friends helped me move past the first four to reach acceptance.

Silence helped me make sense of my new world. Silence allowed me time to think and process.

I had read Edward de Bono's book *The Six Thinking Hats* just a few months before the stroke. The book outlined a method of systemically looking at a situation from multiple perspectives. De Bono explained that "hats" represent different angles from which to view many problems. These angles are such concepts as looking at the big picture, teasing out the facts, recognizing intuitive emotional feelings, applying cautious and conservative logic, optimist benefit identification, and seeking provocative creativity. "Thinking is the ultimate human resource," said de Bono.[2] I was beginning to agree with that statement. Looking at my situation from all possible angles helped me figure out a pathway in this new world. I was constructing the mental or spiritual creation before I dealt with my life's physical recreation. Silent thinking was all I had. The ability to think in silence was perhaps a tender mercy. A tender mercy is a good event in one's life that is not merely a coincidence, but rather is evidence of a loving Savior sending a personal message of comfort. When applied to this dire situation, because my ability to think and have conscious thought was preserved, I had the ability to plan my response to the situation I was in.

I spent a great deal of time pondering important questions about God, His plan for His children, and my plans for myself. What if that small spark could lead to an explosion, a "big bang," leading to the possibility of life evolving in a positive spiral of healing and adaptation, leading to the possibility of me getting *my* life back? I was looking at things from all perspectives, trying to make sense of the stroke and so much more. Could the act of listening to God allow me to conquer my own mind and gain the courage, strength, and foresight to improve my dire situation and help me have a meaningful life?

Listening in silence also permitted me to ask other fundamental questions, questions it was necessary for me to reconcile in my mind: "Why does God allow bad things to happen?" and "Could there be a higher meaning and purpose to suffering?" To answer these, I found myself contemplating the nature of God and our relationship with Him and Jesus Christ.

As a man of faith, but also of science, I thought about our relationship with God in the context of the laws of nature, the human body, and my medical training. I believe not only that you can be both a man of faith and a man of science, but that only in exploring the mysteries of faith and science can one be a truly authentic human being—able to digest truth in all its forms, able to comprehend how all truth is compounded into one complete whole. Silence allowed me to ponder this. There is power in pondering, like a person who has enjoyed snorkeling in the past but has now decided to try scuba diving. But that decision was forced upon me during my time in the hospital, my time being silent before God. However, that time allowed me to dive deeply into my understanding of the gospel and, in turn, the gospel penetrated deeply into my life. Silence may have forced me to spend the time to dive deep and gain a different perspective than I had previously had.

I looked back to my own education—secular, medical, and spiritual. I knew about the laws of nature and also about the nature of our wonderful, but very human bodies. In my medical training, I found it was important to have a keen sense of the human body's frailty. As I studied to gain this understanding, I also realized it was important to keep myself emotionally detached from the cadavers I studied to cope with the uneasiness of working with the body. It wasn't long before I started to see cadavers not as once living, breathing humans, but as a pathology to be studied. As such, I allowed myself to intellectually devour this part of my training.

But I also knew my body was subject to the same natural laws as each cadaver and patient I studied. I cannot detach myself from the small, but substantial and unique knowledge of the body and the mind's workings. Our bodies and minds are not perfect; they are subject to injury, illness, and death when we fall from ladders, when the regulatory systems in our cells malfunction causing cancerous tumors, or when any other natural laws and forces act on them.

But what about God's power to control all things in heaven and on earth? Shouldn't He have power over these natural laws and forces acting on our bodies and minds? Should He shield us from afflictions? In the setting of tragedy, we often wonder about God's role, His love, and

His power. Engulfed in the silence of the stroke, I contemplated these questions again and again.

An injury to the brain, such as occurs with stroke, can damage many functions we consider unique to humans. The brain controls all personality, memory, reason, and judgment. Indeed, man's "soul" can be thought of as the result of complex and remarkable processes in the brain, modified by an elegant cascade of neurotransmitters. Often with a stroke, damage to a portion of the brain happens silently, with little to no outward signs of injury or distress. Historically, this lack of distress caused people to assume the damage caused by a stroke was God's doing or will. They, like us today, wondered about the seemingly senseless calamities that befall the innocent. Strokes affect the old, the young, men, women, sinners and saints; nearly 800,000 people per year suffer strokes in the United States alone. I now care for many of these fine people. It is difficult to imagine that a loving Heavenly Father is responsible for all their hardship.

Rabbi Harold Kushner, in his book *When Bad Things Happen to Good People*, offers this valuable insight. He explains that God agreed to grant us the opportunity for this mortal life and perhaps has relinquished some power to enable us to act and choose for ourselves. He said, "Our misfortunes are none of His doing, and so we can turn to Him for help…not to be judged or forgiven, but to be strengthened and comforted."[3]

Kushner goes on to say, "We can be angry at what has happened to us, without feeling that we are angry at God.... Instead of feeling that we are opposed to God, we can feel that our indignation is God's anger at unfairness working through us, that when we cry out, we are still on God's side, and He is still on ours."[4]

I was a little angry and confused. I did not understand why this stroke had happened to me. But as I pondered Kushner's words, I began to think of our Heavenly Father and Jesus Christ in this light. God was no longer the controller of my afflictions; rather, He was that Being who hath borne our afflictions and grief, my afflictions and grief. I was able to view God not as the Organizer of my suffering, but rather as the champion of my cause and eventual recovery. Though I was not loud and outspoken by nature, being forced to be silent was a painful, yet rare and unique opportunity for me. As I pondered in silence, the answers came, not all at once, but little by little, as the dew from heaven. Although I wanted to cry out and be heard, I found as I listened that Jesus was still listening to me as well. He could hear the songs I could not sing at every point along the journey between two gardens. I came to understand that we are here on earth in very imperfect bodies, interacting with other very imperfect mortals, yet God's ability to support our earthly progress and to ultimately redeem us is perfect. For the rest of my life, as will be seen, I would explore the mystery of that redemption.

CHAPTER 4

EXPLORING CHRIST, THE HEALER

At the time of my stroke, my father, who was then a member of the LDS Church's presiding bishopric, came immediately to my side from Salt Lake City. He was emotionally distraught to see me, his once-lively, beloved son, in such an incapacitated state in the ICU. He has told me several times since how he yearned to have an answer to the question, "Why has this tragedy befallen my son, and not myself, a sixty-five-year-old man?" In my mute state, two-way communication was impossible between us. My father later said to me, "I wish it was me, not you, and although I struggle to know the reasons 'why not me,' I have to have faith that the answers will come and that there *is* a reason." I knew the desire to trade places with me was a true outpouring of my father's love and faith.

After staying with me in the hospital for ten days, my father had to return to Salt Lake for a few days. Although he had given me several blessings during our time together, now he, the father I looked up to, was in need of the comfort of a "priesthood" blessing, a specific ritual in the LDS faith. He sought this comfort from me before he went to the airport. He said he needed reassurance that a reason for my suffering would indeed eventually come. Knowing I couldn't utter a word, my father sat by my side and asked me just to think of the blessing's words.

I did what he requested, neither of us knowing if anyone had ever given a blessing this way before. But our faith was strong, and I was honored that he would reach out to me, his son, to exercise my priesthood in this manner.

As I laid my hands upon his head, picking my limp right arm up with my left arm, and proceeded to think the words in the blessing, I realized I was not even capable of thinking in the context of actual words, though the thoughts were indeed present.

I proceeded to muster up all the love I had to give, hands on head, in silence. Silent in word, silent in thought, but articulate in immortal spirit. My father and I absolutely know that the priesthood power worked through me to bless him that day.

I have never experienced a more powerful representation of the love shared between our Father in Heaven and Jesus Christ than I did in that moment with my father. Feeling just a sliver of this love to and from a father and son was a tender mercy of the Lord.

Years later, we know, as we knew then, that Jesus Christ understood that prayer—that "song unsung"—not in the context of any earthly language, but in the silence that it was. Jesus provided "messianic intercession on our behalf"[1] in peace and the courage to carry on. This experience gave us both insight into the language of love that, perhaps, our Heavenly Father uses to speak to our souls. In a powerful and intimate way, we came to understand better that God indeed has ears to hear the prayers that transcend language. A few days later, when my father returned to Chicago, he seemed to have received the answer he sought. Still in my mute state, he told me he believed that, with time, I would accomplish great things in medicine, in *spite* of the stroke and *because* of the stroke. "I just want to be alive to see it," he said, "because it may take a number of years. The Lord works on a different timeline than us—we both need to have faith in God's purposes." From that point, we both had faith that Christ would heal me...and would do so providing healing sufficient for my needs.

Strokes, accidents, and sometimes death are part of the conditions set out for us in this mortal experience—the general conditions we agreed upon before we entered this world. Christ has a central role to comfort and succor us in times of need, to lead us as a shepherd away from the dangers, and to provide comfort for us in life's storms. Apostle Dale G. Renlund explains, "As the Good Shepherd, Jesus Christ views disease in His sheep as a condition that needs treatment, care, and compassion. This shepherd, our Good Shepherd, finds joy in seeing His diseased sheep progress toward healing."[2]

Perhaps, *even though* we struggle, we carry boundless potential, made possible *because we struggle*. I began to think of my own mortality as an ascent, emotionally and spiritually, not the physical deterioration I was experiencing with my body. I began to echo the words of Paul in Philippians 4:13 when he said, "I can do all things through Christ who strengthens me." Through the silence, I came to know that Christ was present in my life, feeling my pain and giving me strength. And He would provide comfort, strength, and healing if I would turn to Him in faith. Being challenged can be a blessing, or it can be simply a trial. We can find the meaning in struggles or even in pain and suffering, if we have the strength to choose it.

Author Fiona Givens gives further insight into the Savior's ability to heal. She explains that the translators of the King James Bible had to choose between the Greek word *soter*, to *save*, and the word *sodzo*, to *heal* (as He healed the blind man and the hemorrhaging woman). "In all these and numerous other cases, the word often translated as *save* is more aptly rendered *heal*.... In other words, rather than render the Messiah's title of *soter* as *Savior*, we could with equal linguistic justification call him Jesus Christ, Son of God, *Healer* of the world."[3]

Jesus often used disease as a metaphor for hardship, whether it was due to the mortal conditions we face or due to transgression. Whatever the cause of hardship, whether it is due to conditions of mortality or sin, His divine role is to heal our minds of discouragement and despair, or to heal "the mind, not the body, that leads us into sin."[4] Our human minds are what most need healing. Although both the body and the mind occasionally need healing, the mind is the center of choice; it has free-agency (the ability to choose), can comprehend the eternal plan, and provides a breadth of responses to circumstances, situations, and stimuli. If the mind is healthy, or even sanctified, it can control the body to take us out of situations that could lead to our destruction.

However, it may be, in our honest human yearnings, a misunderstanding of priesthood power to expect that man, even a righteous priesthood holder, can dictate the Lord's will. As Apostle Dallin H. Oaks explains, "From all of this we learn that even the servants of the Lord, exercising His divine power in a circumstance where there is sufficient faith to be healed, cannot give a priesthood blessing that will cause a person to be healed if that healing is not the will of the Lord. As children of God, knowing of His great love and His ultimate knowledge of what is best for our eternal welfare, we trust in Him."[5] That sometimes means letting the Lord steer our ship, trusting He will guide us in ways serving His loving purposes. It is more important that the mind draw closer to sanctification than the body be completely healed. The Lord is less concerned about us making a "full recovery" in our bodies, and more concerned with what is best for the eternal welfare of his children. In this sense, I have come to learn that a full recovery means we have the capacity to live a full life. Perhaps our mortal minds are what need healing, healing from pain, fear, and doubt.

I am indeed thankful for the healing I received. Although I have not received a full physical recovery, my recovery is still miraculous and remarkable, and I have made a physical recovery sufficient for my needs. Perhaps more importantly, I have been healed spiritually. I can truly say, as the woman with the issue of blood for twelve years who wanted to touch the garment of the Healer, "my faith hath made me whole." (Matthew 9:20-22). I now trust the Lord to steer my ship, and, perhaps, because of my work, effort, and toil, today I am a more effective servant of the Lord.

About one week after my stroke, I was sent to another hospital to prepare to enter Inpatient Rehabilitation. I was becoming more medically stable, but I was still not showing any signs of neurologic recovery. My family chose Resurrection Hospital on Chicago's outskirts for my rehabilitation because I had been doing my internship there for the last six months. I already had a medical family from my work there, though now I would be going back not to work alongside, but to be treated and cared for by that family. I was coming back in the worst shape possible to occupy the patient rooms where I had been providing care just weeks before. My family chose Resurrection Hospital because they knew I was going to need a strong support system of healthcare providers who truly cared about me, who knew me from before this craziness, who would nurture me back to life for the foreseeable future.

The power of speech still completely escaped me and would for many weeks. How frustrating it was not to be able to relay my feelings to my family. After many days being alone with my thoughts in my mute state, at a time when I was obviously in need of good communication, I yearned to have that connection through speech. I eventually figured out how to write, "I love you" to my dear Emi. With this simple phrase, written to the one who meant the most to me, the communication gap, which had been wide as the oceans, started to become a little narrower, even though we sat side-by-side on the same hospital bed. With tears flowing, we were one step closer together—language is the great connector of hearts.

As my ability to generate very simple, written phrases gradually returned, I wrote down what I had been yearning to express. Simply, "I am OK"—okay with my life, okay with my fate. Communication became possible, but it was still like trying to communicate through a string can telephone over a wide abyss. Then I wrote the content of my heart, forged from days of deliberations and mental turmoil and struggle, second only in importance to my expression of love to Emi, in these six words: "Consider the lilies of the field."

We read in Matthew 6:30, "Consider the lilies of the field, how they grow; wherefore, if God so clothe the grass of the field, shall he not much more clothe you, O ye of little faith?" I was familiar with these verses from a song titled "Consider the Lilies of the Field" authored by Roger Hoffman, which I had sung many times twelve years before in my high school choir. It talks of children who suffer in this world, yet Christ clothes the lilies of the field. Why was I doubtful or worried? Why do any of us not trust in Him to heal our wounds and allow joy and peace back into our lives? I dwelt on this song during the early days after my stroke, but it wasn't until this moment when I could gather my language abilities to write those six words that I realized how much they had come to mean to me. To me, that short phrase meant that "man is never left completely alone, abandoned to his own resources.... God is taking part in his life and destiny."[6]

The deep internalization and realization of this simple verse had a profound effect on me during my weeks of silence and on through today. For me, it caused a hard "reset," allowing me to examine all of my worries, pain, and fear. The choice to give all these things away also meant these gnawing emotions went away. As I let go, these emotions gave rise to courage, faith, and strength in Christ. To have Christ steering my ship, at least for the time being, was a precious treasure. Perhaps for the first time, I was beginning to feel God's love for me because I am His Child, not because of some resume I spent my life working on. The love of God was a treasure more precious than gold. This treasure was made manifest through His own support of me personally, and also manifest in the good and loving ways others supported me. Out of intense anguish, struggles, and silence, the Spirit revealed to me that a loving Heavenly Father is watching over us, intimately and intently.

I reflected on the Savior's suffering, both for our redemption and for our sorrows and afflictions. I felt great gratitude for Christ. Jesus said, "These things I have spoken unto you, that ye might have peace. In the world ye shall have tribulation: but be of good cheer; I have overcome the world" (John 16:33).

I knew at that time, more than at any time previous, that if we stay close to Christ and lean on Him, He will strengthen us, for His grace is sufficient. Because of His gift of strength and example, we, too, can rise from the ashes of our trials. And because of His gift of the Atonement, eventually we, too, will overcome the world. This does bring peace, and we can be of good cheer, even amid tribulation, for we can live in Christ, here and now. I wrote another message to Emi, my family, and to my loved ones—relayed in my mute state, as if communicating from another dimension; the message was simply this: "Surprise Comeback."

Long before the Garden of Eden, long before the world was formed, it seems that God was busy creating the building blocks of our natural world. Before the existence of our sun, stars were formed, and with intense heat and pressure in those suns, fusion reactions took place to form the elements that eventually came together to form our sun, our world, and even our bodies. And, if God so clothed the grasses of the field, of course, He is going to have intense interest in each of us. Our progression increases His glory, and, we, in turn, feel His love in our hearts. We are, in fact, made from celestial materials—our mortal bodies are just too poorly equipped to recognize and comprehend it.

Albert Einstein said, "There are only two ways to live your life. One is as though nothing is a miracle. The other is as though everything is."[7] The way the planets and the earth orbit, the way our own bodies work and can be healed, and the way a loving Heavenly Father watches out for us are absolute miracles we can see every day.

Armed with this awareness of God's love for and interest in me, I realized I was here to work, mortal frailties aside. However, the magnitude of the work for recovery was immense. I could not speak, walk, or take care of my most basic needs. Very basic and practical questions still remained. I didn't know whether I would end up needing an electric wheelchair, a manual wheelchair, or I would regain the ability to walk on my own. I didn't know if I would ever be employed again. But I had faith. My work became more focused, based on fidelity to a higher purpose. It didn't feel like the anxious rat-race of my past, and I was afforded the opportunity to work just on what mattered most—my recovery. Little by little, piece by piece, I was taking back my life, a second life, and the Lord gave me wings.

I later laboriously wrote out the lines of Robert Frost's poem, "Stopping by Woods on a Snowy Evening" because, like the speaker of his poem, I was living in solitude and isolation, though mine were because of communication barriers. I knew I must fight my way back to a world with other people, responsibilities, and obligations.

> The woods are lovely, dark and deep.
> But I have promises to keep,
> And miles to go before I sleep,
> And miles to go before I sleep.[8]

Those words resonated with me then, and they resonate with me now. I recognized that I had miles to go to recover my lost abilities, and I promised myself I would. I would take what was left and live it properly.

The poet Mary Oliver said, "How shall there be redemption and resurrection unless there has been a great sorrow? And isn't the struggle and *rising* the real work in our lives?"[9]

These words took on special meaning for me as I struggled to regain my previous capacities, but I did so with a firm understanding that God was on my side and with a reverence for the Savior and His resurrection.

Could there be a resurrection before a physical death? Paul seems to think so when he says, "I am crucified with Christ: nevertheless, I live, but Christ liveth in me: and the life which I now live in the flesh I live by the faith of the Son of God, who loved me, and gave himself for me" (Galatians 2:20). Professor and author Adam S. Miller explains, "Redemption and even resurrection aren't just for the next life. They can also be part of this life and these bodies, here and now."[10] Perhaps our Heavenly Father would like all humankind to surrender themselves, willingly, to be redeemed. Christ invites all to share in His Resurrection and to have Him present in our lives."[11]

Perhaps the Catholic leaders named their hospital Resurrection Hospital to suggest this invitation from Christ. Not for a promised future resurrection, but to suggest that we consider "if God so clothe the grass of the field…shall He not clothe you, O ye of little faith…But seek ye first the kingdom of righteousness; and all these things shall be added unto you. Take therefore no thought for the morrow: for the morrow shall take thought for the things itself" (Matthew 6:30, 33-34). Paul suggests that we can share in Christ's resurrection by turning over all worry about our future and devoting our lives, as disciples, to Christ. We can be alive in Christ in the present. This is what the name "Resurrection Hospital" has come to mean to me: an opportunity to have us, as individuals, share in Christ's resurrection, become new creatures, and surrender our worldly cares.

Whatever the case, I find it significant that I was brought back to life after my stroke at a place called Resurrection. With this new life, I had new function and new purpose on my journey, between two gardens.

CHAPTER 5

DOING THE HARD THINGS

On September 12, 1962, John F. Kennedy gave an inspirational speech, attempting to rouse a nation to accomplish a seemingly impossible task, "We choose to go to the moon in this decade, and to do the other hard things, not because they are easy, but because they are hard, because that goal will serve to organize and measure the best of our energies and skills. Because that challenge is one that we are willing to accept."[1]

Almost forty years later, in another time of deep resolve in our nation, the season after 9/11, my stroke occurred. At that time, the whole world seemed to be changing. The nation was shrouded in an air of suspicion, and our nation's sense of security and safety had been threatened. George W. Bush gave an equally inspiring speech in which he said, "terror attacks can shake the foundations of our biggest buildings, but they cannot touch the foundation of America.... And I pray [that we will] be comforted by a Power greater than any of us, spoken through the ages in Psalms 23, 'Even though I walk through the valley of the shadow of death, I fear no evil, for You are with me.'"[2]

My stroke, my biggest challenge, occurred on the sixtieth anniversary of the attack on Pearl Harbor, "a day that will live in infamy" for our nation and for me personally. Recovery from that stroke, I soon realized, was going to be as daunting as going to the moon and as frightening as 9/11. Yet it could be overcome with courage. In my case, it was not a nation's task; it was my and my family's task alone to overcome. Emi and I took on the task of doing the required hard things with courage and faith. Those hard things included recovering and living with whatever challenges arose, which would include physical, emotional, and spiritual recovery. The hard work of recovery would take teamwork, cooperation, and a division of labor—over a lifetime.

We had to take things one day at a time. Initially, I lay for hours upon hours in my ICU bed not able to do much of anything. I had a stream of visitors and well-wishers with whom I could not communicate. My doctors ran various tests and scans on me—the same kinds of tests I would've been administering and observing had these been typical days in my internship. This was typical of life in the ICU, but now I was on the other side of the curtain.

Upon seeing my MRI brain scans for the first time, even as a young (and inexperienced) doctor I noticed big white patches over the primary language center and the muscle control "strip" that controls the body's entire right side. I knew what those patches meant—everything I had valued in my once healthy body was gone. I was literally seeing my own brain damage. I fully comprehended it. I felt like how I imagine King Louis XVI of France did immediately after his decapitation, during the several long moments he still had lucidity—his head raised up to the crowd, being able to see his body on the guillotine—before unconsciousness snuffed out the spark of his mortal existence. In my ICU bed, I briefly had visualization, through MRI images on retinas that still functioned, projected to a brain with neurons still firing, of what my life possibilities could entail. I was facing an uncertain future with partial brain loss.

At that moment, I knew that living would be the harder option. Dying may have actually been much easier. On the one hand, like Louis XVI, I could wait until my corpse-like body perished, even though it might take decades, instead of seconds, for decay to overtake it, or I could work through the seemingly impossible challenges that awaited me, to reobtain my life and livelihood. I chose to do the hard things. I chose to live. I was grateful to have this choice, and confident enough in myself and God's assistance to heal my broken body. I was determined to continue living.

My dictum became reclaiming what was lost—essentially a rebirthing process—and having the courage and fortitude to figure out what needed to be done and then executing the strategies that would lead to that plan's achievement. While in the hospital, including the two weeks in the ICU and on the medical floor and the six weeks I spent as an inpatient on the Rehabilitation Unit, I was guided by health professionals through the recovery process. I was eventually discharged from the inpatient setting and was glad to be home with my wife and my baby girl, Ella, even though so much had changed in the last couple of months.

Once I was home and finally out of the hospital, I began going to outpatient therapy on a daily basis. It often took a sense of purpose and resiliency to keep going without the rehab team's formal guidance and structure constantly around me. And there was still a significant communication barrier, even between me and Emi.

I had an arrangement worked out where I received three sessions of formal therapy each weekday and then was able to use the equipment in the outpatient therapy gym for a few hours to get additional practice. I worked on speech and language, arm and hand function, walking, gait mechanics, trotting, pool therapy, jumping, and eventually, jogging. Therapy became my full-time job for several months; it also felt more natural because the outpatient therapy was at Resurrection Hospital, where I had been a medical intern.

During this time, I came to understand more about language: first, the lack of language, then the struggle for basic communication, and then finally, the often profound difficulty of interpersonal connection through language. This last element, the difficulty with interpersonal connection, exists whether you have a language impairment or not.

I felt an urgency to regain speech and communication. I worked intently in outpatient speech therapy. It was necessary for me to go back to the most basic building blocks of verbal communication: single syllables. Forming the lips, tongue, and vocal cords to produce simple sounds, like "ma," and being able to differentiate this sound from the vocal-cord-induced sound of "pa" was a difficult and eye-opening experience. I relearned and practiced all the basic sounds in the English language, much as I had done years before when learning and practicing the sounds for the Japanese language as a nineteen-year-old LDS missionary because I yearned to share the gospel in the Japanese language. Soon, single sounds turned into multi-syllable words that I practiced through halting conversations with therapists, family members, and friends. I enhanced my vocabulary of words I could form by reading children's books aloud, then graduated to more age-appropriate reading.

Through all of this effort, I gained a deep appreciation that the intersection of the physical universe and human emotion and passion lies in language; to love language is to love this intersection. Only when I had language stripped from me could I fully appreciate and understand this concept. Indeed, the loss of language was the most frustrating aspect of having a left-brain stroke. It is strange to be talking normally one minute, and the next, to be unable to operate your tongue and scarcely phonate. But I came to realize that value existed in focusing all of my energy on merely listening. Listening is, perhaps, the critical element in most interpersonal communication. Being forced to listen intently, like I was, was a rare opportunity. Likewise, because of my halting speech, others had to listen intently to communicate with me. This effort sometimes allowed for some even deeper interpersonal communication since both parties had to focus on what the other was saying. Perhaps we can all learn to pay a little more attention in simple face-to-face interactions, in this world of ever-present distractions and things that constantly compete for our attention.

Writing is another vital piece of communication that didn't come without its struggles. My first words written on the computer keyboard were "Steve reads books about mountains." It took me half an hour, which was categorically different than the fifty words per minute I was accustomed to typing. The letters felt so foreign to me. I have come to appreciate that letters and words are really just symbols we use to translate thoughts into something we can communicate to others—sometimes with simplicity, sometimes with great elegance, and yet other times with great subtlety. That I wrote about myself in the third person in that first sentence says a lot about my role after my stroke vs. my previous role of successful medical resident and steady husband and father that I so badly longed to return to. I see now that I had a hard time accepting that this is who I was, here and now.

Eight weeks later, typing words became easier, and I relearned the essentials of the keyboard. As far as spoken language, I tried all manner of things—reading aloud, singing, saying nursery rhymes, attempting to sing karaoke—all in an effort to get my brain circuitry working again.

With time, although my speech remained halting and labored, I gained the ability to speak with others, even holding some simple conversation. I realized, however, that to be an active member of society, and an effective doctor, public speaking was necessary, at least occasionally, so I had a long way to go.

When my brother-in-law Chad was going to serve a two-year LDS mission, he invited me to speak at his farewell service in church. Chad and Emi's parents' home church congregation had been very generous to Emi and I in sharing not just words of encouragement, but also through financial donations as we tried to get back on our feet. For this reason, I felt additionally prompted to address this group that had shown so much love. Just six months after the stroke, as emotionally challenging as it was, I knew I had to express my appreciation. I felt I needed to do it, and in a sense, I wanted to do it. I knew doing so would put my deficits on exhibit, but I would swallow my pride and show the new Steve Edgley, the person I had become after my rebirth—and publicly face an uncertain future.

I had learned that public speaking and language are powerful and crucial ways to connect with the rest of humanity. I needed that form of connection to be a part of my future. My walk up to the pulpit was short. I began speaking, one word at a time, with awkward deliberateness. I addressed Chad, who would be going on to the missionary training center to receive specialized training for many hours a day. I told the congregation I would be leaving for Alabama to receive some specialized training for a different purpose, stroke recovery, which would also be for many hours a day. I said, though thousands of miles away from each other, I would draw on Chad's strength as he drew on mine. "I don't know why this happened to me," I said, "but I have faith through Christ who strengthens me" (Philippians 4:13).

As an aside, over the last decade or so, I have been able to provide medical care for several of the people in Chad's home church congregation who so generously provided us with donations and support in our hour of need so many years ago. I feel it's been a sacred, cherished privilege to do so as they occasionally encounter life's severe challenges. I am honored to help them walk back into the light again, or, more rarely, provide care for them as they make the transition from this life to the next.

After my talk before Chad's congregation, I still felt uneasy about exposing myself through public speech. However, I knew it was an important step toward the things I wanted to do and the person I wanted to be. This experience wasn't a profound spiritual experience. Nonetheless, I now recognize that the power and courage to do this small and seemingly insignificant thing and to take many more small steps throughout my recovery process came from the enabling and strengthening power of Jesus Christ's Atonement.

Just a few years after speaking at Chad's farewell, I was invited to speak at my first national medical conference in Park City on emerging techniques in stroke rehabilitation. After approaching the pulpit and doing the obligatory A/V microphone check, "Can you hear me in the back?" a man called out and said, "We can hear you; we just can't understand you."

Jerk, I thought to myself…but then I was able to press on. Though still far from perfect in speech, I now know who it is who strengthens me. Needless to say, I have now spoken to local and national audiences dozens of times.

Doing the hard things sometimes requires ingenuity. As I worked to recover, I thought a lot about the space missions, including overcoming disaster in the space program. I contemplated the Apollo 13 mission, launched in April 11, 1970, only to be aborted due to an oxygen tank explosion. Getting the three astronauts safely back to earth required heroic and masterful planning and execution. Miraculously, through the efforts of many bright and talented people, they were brought home successfully.

I was hoping for a similar miracle, not to get me back to earth, but to find a way back into the field of medicine and a semblance of my former life. Much like the NASA engineers and astrophysicists, I needed to assess the situation, figure out what tools and resources I still possessed, and maximally use those tools and resources. I realized that learning a foreign language had probably developed a brain circuitry in me that would enable the return of my language capability, with time and great effort. I realized my former athletic endeavors would serve me well as I relearned how to perform the simplest of tasks. I also realized a whole cadre of people, with their own assistance and resources, were waiting in the wings, anxious to help. I could not panic or quit; I had to work steadily and with purpose. Indeed, I echoed Paul's words, "I therefore run, not as uncertainly; so fight I, not as one that beateth the air" (1 Corinthians 9:26). Such was my mission. I realized I didn't have time or energy to wallow in self-pity. There would be mid-flight adjustments, I was sure of that. I might even need to splash down on the other side of the world, as was the case in the Apollo 13 mission. If it would take me changing medical fields and extensive adaptations, that's what I would do, for I was a new man. I *could* do this. I *would* do this.

In this period of recovery, I did many things that confused the people around me, including those closest to me. It was just so hard to explain myself in detail, including to the people who probably needed explanations the most.

On one trip to visit my in-laws in Salt Lake City, I noticed a bucket of Brio railroad parts, a young child's toy, in their home. Still in intense therapy for my hemiparetic right arm and leg, I realized that toy was the therapy tool I was looking for. For a couple of hours each day, I assumed various positions on the floor working with the toy set. Picking up the railway pieces with my right hand, supporting my weight while sitting on the floor with my right arm, and working on trunk control was very important to my recovery process, even though to the outside observer, I was merely playing with a child's toy. Assembling the tracks in a design was an appropriate visuospatial cognition exercise as well. I had a finite amount of time to regain my lost abilities, or so I thought, before people forgot about the Steve Edgley who was an aspiring doctor. As such, I was willing to do whatever it took to regain my former abilities, even if only in small increments. I had to be willing to do hard, and sometimes humiliating, things.

While on that same trip to Salt Lake City, we stopped at my boyhood home, where my parents still live. There I decided to make hard candy suckers. Hard candy making and selling was a main source of income for me when I was ten or eleven. My parents thought it quite quaint and childlike for their adult son to pull out old sucker molds and proceed to make candy. However, I was very interested in the challenge of remembering and following the recipe, and in physically testing myself, with only one working hand, to see if I could complete the task. It may have been somewhat humiliating, but I had to be willing to do the hard things (and in this case, the results were delicious).

About six months after my stroke, one of my therapists learned of an advanced recovery technique called constraint-induced movement therapy (CIMT). A multicenter research study was enrolling stroke patients with similar stroke characteristics as me, and we determined the intense therapy would be good for my recovery. The idea with CIMT is to put patients in an environment where they are required to do everything with their impaired limb (in my case, my right arm and hand). Patients are immersed in that environment, with their healthy limb restrained so they have to use the impaired limb. The main site of the study was in Birmingham, Alabama. Emi and I determined it would not be practical for her to go with and assist me while caring for our one-year old baby, Ella. Instead, my dear mother was willing to come with me. We flew together and checked into the hotel where we would stay for sixteen days. I was driven to do all I could to regain function—even if this new therapy failed, I knew it was important at least to try. A large component of this form of therapy is the restraining of the good, functional arm, thereby forcing you to use your impaired arm. The concept is sound: goal-directed, task-specific, repetitive practice, eight hours per day for two weeks. I knew this type of intense therapy would be good for my hand and arm function recovery. It was the steady, sustained, and complete immersion I felt I needed.

I did not anticipate, however, the physical and emotional toll it would take. This toll, in part, was due to being in a new setting, without my usual support, with my young family seemingly torn apart. The therapy was also grueling. A large part of the anguish those recovering from a stroke, trauma, or medical event experiences stems from our interpersonal relationships—the emotional weight and pressure we feel as a result of trying to connect with people in our sphere of influence. Yet we yearn for this deep love, connectivity, and concern for others. However, on the other side of that same coin is the potential to experience deep anguish for the people we care about. Certainly, this pain, borne of deep love and concern, was one element the Savior felt in the Garden of Gethsemane. Perhaps, on this earth, the ability to feel anguish for loved ones is both a burden we develop and a godly characteristic.

At the end of this two-week period of intense therapy, my hand and arm function was marginally better; however, my progress was less than I desired. Although I relearned how to use my shoulder, elbow, and wrist more effectively, yielding great dividends in the ensuing years, my hand function did not improve nearly to the point I had hoped. I had lofty goals for my hand to regain the function needed to operate surgically, but after this treatment, I could perform only simple grasp-and-release activities and was unable even to move my fingers independently of one another. Nevertheless, any improvement was welcomed and valuable to me. And although I did not improve to the point I wished, my arm and hand function did improve. The study showed that most patients have had significant success with this therapy, including myself, though most patients are not able to achieve 100 percent full recovery of their hands. Still, the CIMT principles that stemmed from this study form an important and valuable component of the therapy we use in the outpatient clinic where I work today.

Unfortunately, in this space between two gardens, we cannot make the tissue of our brains whole again by our own power. In spite of neuroscience and plasticity (the brain's ability to change itself), once an area of the brain is damaged, the tissue does not miraculously grow back and restore itself. Humans can go to the moon and back, but we can't fix the brain. Once an area of the brain becomes damaged, the brain's other parts have some capacity to make up for the damaged tissue, but this capacity is limited. While every portion of the brain is responsible for an important function, some areas are more critical to the function of what we highly value. These highly specialized regions are called eloquent tissue. For example, almost 50 percent of stroke patients lose dexterity in their affected hand, which represents a loss of eloquent tissues. A person can often bring back some function in eloquent tissue (sometimes called restoration of latent potential). However, this recovery, although significant, is usually incomplete.

Because of these irreversible changes in my brain, I literally became a new creature. I will likely always have an impaired right hand, and my speech will likely always be slightly halting. Such are the mortal body's limitations.

Perhaps in a more profound and hopeful way, we can become new creatures as our spirits heal. If a person devotes himself to Christ, even though human and subject to mortal frailties, "he is a new creature: old things are passed away; behold, all things are become new" (2 Corinthians 5:17). I believe this is what is meant by being saved by grace and being spiritually born again. Sometimes, we will fail in our attempts at the hard things, even after all we can do, but His grace is always sufficient. As opposed to what man can do, even with the assistance of science, the gospel's essence is that a fundamental and permanent spiritual change in our very nature is possible. This change doesn't bring back a hand affected by stroke, but it can fundamentally change what that hand engages in.

Bednar explains that this change in our nature, being born again, requires a "total immersion in and saturation with the Savior's gospel." However, just as my physical recovery was not immediate or quick, Bednar reminds us that spiritual rebirth "does not occur quickly or all at once; it is an ongoing process—not a single event. Line upon line and precept upon precept, gradually and almost imperceptibly, our motives, our thoughts, our words, and our deeds become aligned with the will of God. This phase of the transformation process requires time, persistence, and patience."[3] This transformation is possibly the hardest aspect of healing, and possibly also the most underappreciated, for it is neither easy to perceive or rapid, but if the spirit is willing, there is not much the body cannot do. Conquer the spirit and mind and the body will find meaningful adaptations.

In our world, between two gardens, many do not recognize that the human spirit drives all of human behavior. This fact reinforces the primacy of knowing, not "who we are," but of knowing "from Whom we came," for we are truly the offspring of deity, sons and daughters of God. Our Heavenly Father loves each one of us and will inspire and assist us in this mortal journey in ways that will bring us back to Him. However, many of us fail to recognize or appreciate God's assistance and inspiration if it doesn't meet our immediate needs.

Looking back, this change in my spirit and my nature can be summarized, in part, by the transformation from the desire and striving to be "highly-esteemed" of men and loving the praise of men more than God (see Luke 16:15 and John 12:43) to having a new sense of focusing on obtaining peace and contentment from love in the sight of God. I believe the same is true for others who have gone through a similar situation.

In my youth, specifically in high school, I was a highly devoted and dedicated athlete, playing high school basketball. In a real sense, basketball provided me with the public forum to gain high esteem from others. Also, basketball provided the competitive outlet I needed and an opportunity to work hard at something I thought was very important. At that point, I probably sought the praise of men more than God.

Then, the time came for me to serve as a missionary. I served in Japan with all my heart, immersing myself in the Savior's gospel. I "became a man [and] I put away childish things," (1 Corinthians 13:11), including the praise that comes from man when able to shoot a ball through a basket. I was in the process of transforming into a new being.

When I came back from Japan, I got very serious about my pre-med education, and I did the medical-related service required, in part, to gain the attention of medical schools. Still, in my personal essay, which was part of the medical school application, I wanted to show the medical school how committed I could be, so I made mention of an over-consuming devotion and veneration to an orange basketball hoop set ten feet off the ground. When Dr. Robert Lichtenberg interviewed me at Loyola Medical School in Chicago, he said afterward, "I didn't know if I would be interviewing Michael Jordan or Mother Teresa"—an unnecessarily grandiose response. Over the next few years, serving myself through the rigors of medical education, I forgot the enabling power of immersing myself in the Savior's gospel. When I graduated from medical school and started my medical residency with the goal of becoming an eye surgeon, I spent a lot of energy thinking about the pride I felt in the accomplishments I was so near to obtaining. In fact, before my stroke, in the first year of residency, each morning I spent a brief moment walking from my car through the physicians' parking lot while wondering what model of expensive car I would get. Payoff for my hard work was quickly approaching, and I was going to show the world my accomplishments. Whether this was a form of idolatry or seeking the praise of man, I don't really know. Perhaps it was both. Either way, possessions and the praise of man was in my heart and consuming my precious mental energies.

Perhaps the stroke put the Savior back into my life more fully.

As I have said previously, my belief is that our Heavenly Father doesn't cause life's misfortunes. Rather, trials are the natural consequence of earth's physical environment. When misfortunes arise, it's up to us to decide whether to rely upon the strength of man, or accept His grace, which is the enabling and strengthening power of Christ's Atonement. The Lord can transform our suffering for His purposes. Still, to this day, when I am confronted with a difficult problem, patient issue, or personal issue, I often silently repeat St. Francis of Assisi's prayer, "Lord, make me an instrument of Thy peace." Every time I do this, I feel enabled and strengthened.

The difficulty arises in the fact that, sometimes, true discipleship requires us to reinvent ourselves in order to progress and become a new creature; sometimes we experience this process over and over again. This experience is often difficult, but through the grace of Christ, we can have the strength to change.

Christ's strength is particularly needed at the transitions of life, where discipleship requires a reinvention—moving through the stages of life, from student to single adult, spouse, employee, parent, grandparent, and on and on. With each transition, disciples change to become new creatures, whether slightly or rigorously.

At each juncture and transition, we can choose to strive for the praise of men, even if our outward behavior may suggest otherwise as we "go through the motions." Discipleship thus becomes a matter of the heart. Whom we each serve, whether mammon or the everlasting God, is a choice.

LDS President Spencer W. Kimball explains the moral imperative of choosing the Lord over the praise of man: "To set aside all these great promises in favor of a chest of gold and a sense of carnal security is a mistake in perspective of colossal proportions. To think that he has settled for so little is a saddening and pitiful prospect indeed; the souls of men are far more precious than this."[4] Perhaps this understanding is part of the legacy my father taught me when he chose to serve the Lord and accept the job working for the LDS Church, instead of seeking wealth and men's praise.

Each of us likely has periods of waxing and waning devotion to God, who said "people draw near me with their mouths, with their lips do honor me, but have removed their heart far from me" (Isaiah 29:13). At times, we will give in to the enticing world for a moment. Perhaps by grand design, we are created to find the honor of men attractive, so we have the opportunity to learn to put off these desires and come onto Christ, who will help us to progress. In so doing, we will have our hearts knit in unity with God.

As I attempted to reinvent myself and transition into a new creature, both spiritual and physical changes were certainly required. I was hoping to make a full recovery, and in many ways I did make a spiritual recovery as I learned how this experience could bring me closer to my Heavenly Father. However, as I worked through therapy and recovery's physical aspects, even though my doctors were all pleased with my remarkable progress, it became apparent that my physical recovery would be less than complete. I was disappointed, and I didn't know why the Lord was withholding His blessings from me.

With time, I drew understanding and strength from a subtle lesson in the Savior's life. For example, in all four gospels of the New Testament, Jesus feeds 5,000 people with just five loaves of bread and two fishes. Yet, none of the accounts mentions a miraculous multiplying of the loaves and fishes, just the mention of "And they did all eat, and were filled" (Matthew 14:20), even to the point of there being an overabundance.

Those 5,000 people may not have had a loaf of bread each. But even with the little they were given, they were miraculously filled. Like them, I knew that although there wasn't a miraculous restoration of neural connections to my cells and muscles, I, too, had enough. I learned to recognize that I did progress physically, through my Savior's assistance. My physical recovery was sufficient, as His grace is sufficient… and I was "filled."

However, I realized I would need to make some major adjustments in my life and work. I was advised by my therapist to learn how to take advantage of assistive technology. Voice-to-text technology was just coming out, and I anticipated it would be very useful in assisting me in my return to work as a resident-physician since I didn't have use of my right hand for typing. I would need this technology to document patient histories and physicals and to write progress notes. In learning how to use assistive technology, I was trying to prepare myself for the endless medical documentation in the healthcare field. I wanted to work as efficiently as other residents rather than slowly handwriting with my left hand or typing things out one handed. As I learned this technology, I again recognized the Lord's grace. My mind was miraculously filled with energy to create novel methods of accommodating the physical impairments that remained. As I worked with an assistive technology specialist, learning how to use a speech-to-text program as an effective tool, I gained confidence that I could adapt to my new situation and a busy workplace environment.

Additionally, to mimic the way I was accustomed to rest my other wrist on the paper I was writing on, I learned to secure the paper to a clipboard, complete with a calculator built-in at the board's top. This became a comfort blanket of sorts for my writing activities.

I spent hundreds of hours trying to regain full function of my hand, speech, and body, trying to achieve every ounce of physical recovery I could. I wanted to be healed completely, but after a time, I had to accept that Christ's grace is sufficient and my physical healing was sufficient. Looking back on that time, years later, I am thankful for the lessons and personal growth that have come as a result of my stroke's physical challenges.

Thankfully, this recovery period wasn't all tedious. "In life, if you're not having fun, you're not doing it right," one of my stroke patients told me years later. I decided I needed to have fun during my recovery, so I set a goal to learn to run again. I had run the Chicago Marathon and competed in a few triathlons the year prior to my stroke. Running the Chicago Marathon had been one of the most exhilarating experiences of my life, so I was eager to get back to some sort of competition. After extensive work with my physical therapists, as well as practice on my own, I was able to run effectively, though not at the competitive level of my pre-stroke days. It became an important goal of mine to run a 5K race. I spent about three months in preparation with my physical therapist. I dealt with my post-stroke "foot-slap" and had to concentrate on every foot placement on every step. The therapist helped me with stretching my legs and my doctor placed me on a medication to relax my muscles that were stiff.

The day of the race came, and I went all out. By the race's end, I was utterly exhausted. I had a more difficult time forming words, I was nauseous, and I had immediate diarrhea—my mind and my body were overtaxed and drained. However, in spite of all this, it was good for my confidence.

Although I felt pride in the accomplishment, I realized running would not be an effective form of exercise for me. Even now, I occasionally dream of being able to run and glide effortlessly, but it is just not possible.

Nevertheless, after running this race, I thought I had the endurance and stamina to work the thirty-six-hour shifts residents often had to perform. Returning to medical residency was my main goal, and after this 5K and one year of extensive rehabilitation and retraining, I felt the urgency of completing my medical residency and finally becoming a doctor. I knew the longer I waited, the less likely I was to return to medicine, so I felt I needed to return as soon as possible.

To return to residency successfully, I would need a mass of people on my side, all with the impetus to help me achieve my goal of returning to medicine. Fortunately, I had large scale support, from the hospital's administrative directors to fellow residents and staff. Most notably, I had the support of the residency programs director. However, it was very apparent to everyone that I still had some major hurdles to navigate. Communication was extremely difficult, with both colleagues and patients, and doing essentially everything with my non-dominant left hand was challenging, to put it mildly. However, we'd signed the residency contract, and a date to return to residency had been set for the beginning of December, only about two weeks away.

During those two weeks, a friend from my church congregation, whom I will call Tyler, went missing. During my year of intense stroke recovery and therapy, Tyler had been forced to take a break from his medical school training because of intense struggles with anxiety and depression. His challenges were not physical or language-oriented like mine, but psychological. Over the past year, we had grown closer since we were both out of school and struggling with medical problems. Emi and Tyler's wife, Lucy, were also close because they both worked together in an assignment at our church congregation. We both knew Tyler was really hurting from depression, but, as happens so much of the time, I didn't really know how to help him. Tyler had been counseled to consider other non-medical career options.

One snowy November morning before I was to return to residency, Emi awoke with the strong feeling, or prompting, to "find Lucy." Emi promptly went to Lucy's home, as well as her place of work. When she found that Lucy wasn't at either spot, she again went back to Lucy's home. At that point, Lucy was there. Tyler was missing and had left a goodbye letter. Lucy and Emi called the police. Both the police and many of Tyler and his wife's friends began a search. About two hours after that initial call, the police came to Tyler's apartment. Tyler's body had been found, and he had died. The police officer correctly described Tyler's wedding band to Tyler's wife, a gold ring with three small diamonds. The police officer said, "We need someone to go to the ER to identify him." They suggested it not be Tyler's wife, so Emi and I went to identify the body, with Lucy. We all braced ourselves for the worst.

When we arrived at the ER, we learned a white male had jumped from a sixty-foot overpass and died at the scene. The police needed someone to identify the body. Emi and I were escorted into an ER room, where our friend's body lay supine with a sheet over it. I pulled the sheet down and exposed his face. He had the tell-tale signs of a basal skull fracture, but we knew it was Tyler.

I uncovered his body further. I noticed his wedding ring. I saw his beautifully perfect hands. For a moment I thought, "If he really didn't need them, couldn't I have just one?" However, I knew my limited physical abilities were my cross to carry; Tyler died under the weight of another cross.

Although our challenges were very different, a common thread existed in my and Tyler's challenges. We were both mourning the loss of abilities—and dreams. When a young man marries a young woman and takes her across the country to attend medical school, as Tyler and I had both done, a tacit agreement, a commitment, exists that we are going to make that woman's sacrifice worthwhile. The feeling of a broken commitment—of not being able to provide and protect—is very hard on a young mind. It was hard on Tyler, and it was hard on me.

As I stood, looking at my friend's lifeless body, I realized fully just how hard this course, this soul-straining effort toward the ultimate goal of becoming a doctor, was on me and Emi. I don't really know what made the difference in our outcomes since we had both tried to lean on the Lord's grace and strength.

Human suffering, from stroke, depression, cancer, heart disease, or any number of things our mortal bodies are susceptible to, invariably causes suffering, struggles, and sometimes death. Tyler's tragedy was difficult to understand, but I realized sometimes a person's mental health is even more disabling than physical problems. We are all products of our biology, physiology, and psychology—our mortal bodies. Fortunately, we also have immortal souls, and the power of Christ's atonement to be resurrected with a perfected mind and body.

As strong and robust as we want to believe our bodies are, frail may be a more accurate description, especially when referring to the mind's delicate balances. Perhaps this illusion of strength is too enticing to resist. Even as physicians, we struggle to reconcile this ideal of strength and fortitude with the frailty and death we so often face both with patients and in our personal lives.

Often, physicians in the hospital where I work must wrestle with life and death decisions for patients. How we wrestle with these decisions, and ultimately make them for ourselves, is a major determinant of the kind of doctors we become, how we practice medicine, and how we all practice life.

LDS President Russell M. Nelson, a renowned doctor himself, said, "for all conscientious doctors, death's gateway from life also threatens as a potential gateway to defeat. Realistically, every patient of every doctor, if followed for long enough, will pass away. And when death does occur, a sense of sadness naturally seems to prevail, regardless of the age of the deceased."[5] Whether a person is young or old, whether a death is expected or tragic, death takes its toll on each of us. Dealing with death and coming to understand and appreciate our mortality is one of the hard things not only doctors, but each of us must learn. But, as Anna Quindlen so wisely said, "Knowledge of our own mortality is the greatest gift God ever gave us."[6]

Moving on after a patient or loved one dies requires strength and faith. This strength and faith are accessible to us through Christ's grace. He strengthens us and enables us to recognize our mortality, from the beginning to the end, as a journey to gain experience and progress. If we have faith, we can better recognize how He strengthens us throughout our journey.

I humbly recognize whom I gained my strength from as I recovered and whom I continue to gain strength from every day. Through the Lord's grace, I was able to realize that my battle to recover both physically and mentally was the Lord's battle. This realization gave me tremendous hope and a sense of purpose as I moved forward with my residency.

I restarted residency training as a humble and broken vessel, and I was eager to fulfill that unspoken commitment to provide for and protect my young family—while bearing my own cross. My journey ultimately led me to the field of stroke rehabilitation—with purpose: "I was sick and you cared for me" (Matthew 25:36 NLT). I did this despite my impaired right arm and hand, my speech impediment, and my partial paralysis in my right foot and ankle. These impairments, over time, have become second nature to me. I have attempted to attain a high quality of life, in part through my service as a doctor.

I have seen thousands of stroke patients in my medical practice since my residency. Some patients do better than I have, but some, unfortunately, do worse. Perhaps, faith sufficient to accept the Father's will is the most important factor in recovery. . .and in life.

In a devotional given to young adults, Bednar relates a story of a young cancer patient he knew. Bednar said, despite everything we read about needing the faith to be healed, perhaps what is more important is the faith to submit to the Father's will, whatever the outcome. Bednar asked this young cancer patient if he had the faith "not to be healed."[7] Or, in other words, do each of us have sufficient faith when our preconceived notions don't go our way?

The Lord knows what it is to suffer, for He has felt every form of pain. Thus, He can empathize and succor us as no one else can. His grace strengthens us to be able to do the hard things in life, much more than we could ever do on our own. He comprehends the complete picture, much more than we could ever understand it on our own. Neal A. Maxwell said, "As we confront our own. . .trials and tribulations, we too can plead with the Father, just as Jesus did, that we 'might not. . . shrink'—meaning to retreat or to recoil. Not shrinking is much more important than surviving! Moreover, partaking of a bitter cup without becoming bitter is likewise part of the emulation of Jesus."[8]

Whether we recover fully from an illness or are led down a different path than we had originally planned, I have faith that He is ultimately guiding us and leading us to reach our full potential as children of a loving Heavenly Father. This life is full of hard things—for everyone. However, we can learn and grow from all of life's experiences. And even when walking in the shadow of death, the Savior is with us, on our journey between two gardens.

CHAPTER 6

CHOOSING FAITH AND SEEING TENDER MERCIES

In his speech *You Know Enough*, LDS leader Neil L. Anderson relates a story of a friend whose young daughter was killed in a tragic accident. His friend, in unbearable sorrow, began to question his faith. The friend's wife wrote to Anderson to ask if he would give her husband a priesthood blessing. He said, "As I laid my hands upon his head, I felt impressed to tell him something that I had not thought about in exactly the same way before. The impression that came to me was: Faith is not only a feeling; it is a decision. He would need to choose faith."[1]

After this blessing, Andersen's friend realized he knew enough to move forward, to choose faith. "He got on his knees. His spiritual balance returned."

In this life, we don't always know why bad things happen to us or to those we love. We often don't understand the reason for overwhelming trials. In this mortal space between two gardens, we have a limited ability to see the full picture. And, sometimes, it feels like we are walking alone in the dark. But like the man in this story, we can choose to have faith—faith that we are not alone, that we are loved by God and Jesus Christ, and that each difficult moment will ultimately be for our good. As we choose faith, we can develop within ourselves a glimmer of light, a testimony to guide us, until the full picture is revealed.

Whether your light is as a candle or as the noonday sun, wherever you are on your faith journey, you can and should celebrate and encourage yourself and others to move forward and grow in faith.

However, sometimes we are left in a dark place, seemingly to fend for ourselves. At these times, we can have guidance and courage to go gladly into the dark night. In England, during the dark times of World War II, people gained courage from these lines penned by Minnie Louisa Haskins, called "God Knows":

> And I said to the man who stood at the gate of the year:
> "Give me a light that I may tread safely into the unknown."
> And he replied:
> "Go out into the darkness and put your hand into the Hand of God.
> That shall be to you better than light and safer than a known way."
> So I went forth, and finding the Hand of God, trod gladly into the night.
> And He led me towards the hills and the breaking of day in the lone East.

How much comfort it brings to know that if we put our hand into His hand, God will lead us out of the darkness toward the breaking of day?

For some, or perhaps for all of us at one point or another, it may be difficult to stay on a path of faith, especially when trials and struggles come our way. We may feel overwhelmed or feel as though God has forgotten us. Those moments when our faith feels stretched thin, however, can be the moments when faith grows the most. All we have to do is choose to believe, or even just choose to want to believe. Of all the things that have been written about faith, at the very root of it all, faith is a choice.

For some of us, choosing faith may be challenging because faith isn't something you can test, see, or measure. Faith, by its nature, is a belief in spiritual things—belief in things unseen, instead of a belief in hard facts and scientific proof. Faith is outside the realm of objective observation. However, I have the personal belief that our human capacity for understanding faith and religion will one day be easy for the mind to comprehend objectively, and that the schools of thought, science, and religion will one day meld into one. Nevertheless, the patience that this viewpoint requires, the hope for resolution in some future day, has challenged many people close to me, so much so that some have disavowed religion completely. I believe God created our minds to have the capacity to see things with the objective/scientific lens and the spiritual lens. Our challenge is to meld them into one image, even here and now.

The decision to believe in something you can't see takes a conviction and trust that is hard to understand or articulate. Even though it sometimes seems impossible to reconcile our faith with science and the world around us, when surveyed throughout the world, time and time again, most people choose faith to some degree.[2] We seem to have an innate desire to believe in a Higher Power of some sort because of this inborn yearning to look to the Divine.

I work in an environment where I stand witness to some of life's hardest blows, but I often have the opportunity to see some heroic and miraculous comebacks, as well as some courageous patients who don't recover. One thing each of these heroic stories has in common is that the patients believe in their future and in something beyond themselves.

One morning, after completing rounds for my medical and rehabilitation care patients in the inpatient rehabilitation unit, I went back to talk to and counsel a middle-aged couple. Only days before, the husband had experienced a sudden hemorrhagic stroke; a blood vessel had burst within his brain, rendering him paralyzed on his left side. Imaging scans showed the cause of the bleeding in his brain was actually a tumor. The blood vessels in tumors have a predilection for bursting and bleeding. The tumor would need to be removed. After he recovered enough strength, his neurosurgeons went in to remove the tumor.

After his surgery, this patient returned to the rehabilitation unit. The tumor had been sent to the pathologist to ascertain whether it was benign or aggressive and fatally cancerous. When the pathology results came back, as fate would have it, he was found to have a fairly aggressive malignant tumor.

The oncology team was responsible for sharing this news with the couple, but knowing the pathology results, and because I loved this patient and his family, I wanted to help soften the blow. I knew they would have a long road ahead of them, with weeks of chemotherapy, radiation therapy, and general uncertainty. We talked about my experience with a stroke and empathized over the challenges we both had faced and would face. When I asked this couple if they had religious inclinations, they said, "Sort of...but more so, recently." I told them it has been very important to me to know our lives have a plan and purpose. I told them they had our full support for the duration of the treatment and its aftermath. I also told them I hoped they would be able to feel God's love in all this.

The patient's wife said, "We've actually only been married for two years, but we love each other to death. Your words were exactly what we needed to hear." She went on to say, "It's my feeling that all these difficulties of life will be made up in the next life." They believed. And although they had a different faith than me, their belief helped them navigate this difficult challenge. Their belief was powerful.

Sometimes we forget the power the simple act of believing can have. We get lost thinking faith means something is true or real. Jeffrey R. Holland stated, "*belief* is a precious word, an even more precious act, and [we] need never apologize for 'only believing'...that Christ Himself said, 'Be not afraid, only believe.'"[3] We forget that Christ himself asked us simply to believe in Him.

This couple could have felt forsaken by God when they found out about the husband's cancer, but instead, they believed. I will admit, in my darkest hours during and after my stroke, I had that question, "Why hast thou forsaken me?" (Matthew 27:46). I felt forgotten by God, and I wondered why He had allowed such a devastating stroke to happen.

This feeling of being alone and forgotten by a Being whom I believe loves us and never forsakes us is something I'm sure I have not been alone in feeling. Feeling forsaken by God is a human emotion every one of us may feel at some point. Often, it comes after a major trial in our life or the life of someone close to us. It's a feeling that can usually be traced back to some of our most powerful emotions from what is often called our primitive brain. These three emotions are fear, pain, and anger. We feel all three emotions when we feel forsaken. We feel fearful, and we feel mental pain and often anger when we sense we might actually be alone in the world, in our trials, with nowhere to turn for support and no one watching out for us with a loving hand. We feel the pain of an unfair and unjust world, and we can often languish in self-pity.

It is more difficult to hold on to faith and love when God seems to be the instigator of our suffering. Then it is very different to think of God as a loving Being, guiding us through this mortal classroom. Instead, we may see him as a cruel headmaster doling out hostile, even violent paddling in a school of hard knocks. We all go through times when we feel the misguided temptation to dwell on a sense of abandonment. When the chips don't fall our way, either from wrong choices or merely bad luck—some of which are the conditions of this mortal world—it is all too easy to take that fallacious sense of God's desertion and convert it into rebellion or apathy, rather than following a straight and narrow path. Yet these are precisely the occasions when we need to hold tighter. Certainly, a testimony tempered by experience grows stronger. It's possible, if not likely, that this, too, is by Heavenly design.

Let me share another story of belief in a moment of immense pain that has greatly impacted my life. I relate powerfully to a certain handcart pioneer (pioneers who pulled all their belongings in handcarts across the plains), Francis Webster. When Francis was eighteen, he left his home in England and traveled to many parts of the world, including Australia and New Zealand, and then spent several years prospecting for gold in California. When he returned to England in 1855, he had accumulated enough gold to get a comfortable start to life. But then he met the LDS missionaries, was baptized, and got married. He and his new bride wanted to gather with the saints in Salt Lake City to seek a new fortune and future, with faith.

Francis had the money to ride in the comfort of a horse-drawn wagon, but instead, he chose to join with Edward Martin and his group of handcart pioneers in 1856. Francis paid the passage of nine other pioneers, mostly immigrants from Denmark, who were too poor to pay their way. However, when the company arrived in Wyoming to find heavy snow had already covered the mountains and plains, he and the other members of the Martin handcart pioneer company paid a terrible price. Approximately 200 people died during the journey, and many others suffered from frostbite, amputations, permanent disability, and broken dreams. But one dream remained strong for each of them—to join the saints in Salt Lake. Their faith was strong throughout the journey's horrors. Even in the face of fear, death, and trial, these saints did not lose their belief in Christ. They could have chosen to feel forsaken, forgotten, and angry—but they did not.

I have stood on those shores and docks of Copenhagen and London where many members of the Martin Company departed their homeland, as well as many of my own ancestors (though not as part of the fateful Martin handcart group). And although I may never understand what prompted those pioneers to leave everything—the depth of their emotions, the depth of their desperation—their actions stand as a testament to the measure of their quiet desperation. Risking everything, they found hope and courage to cross a wide ocean and a rugged continent. So desperate was their situation, so strong was their faith, so great was the hope and conviction of their hearts.

Decades after reaching the Salt Lake Valley, when Francis was an old man, he opened up about the ordeal. He said the decision to head out so late in the year was a mistake (made by imperfect mortal men trying to do their best). Nevertheless, he said of the experience, "We suffered beyond anything you can imagine, and many died of exposure and starvation…[but we] came through with the absolute knowledge that God lives, for we became acquainted with Him in our extremities."[4] Instead of dwelling on their fear, anger, and the forsakenness many in the company probably did feel, these faithful Saints chose to believe God was there with them. They chose to become acquainted with Him, even if he felt far away to some. They hoped He was there and would carry them through, and He did.

I, too, can appreciate this measure of desperation with my struggles after my stroke. Though it was a different time, we are all bound by the same basic emotions. The horrendous experiences of Frances Webster remind me, as it reminds us all, that I can never feel like I am the only one who has suffered seemingly pointlessly, or prayed for pain to end, or had their dreams crushed for a time.

Like these early pioneers, *we* may feel burdened by trials, as well. And like I did, we may wonder if God has forgotten us in various moments of our lives. Those moments of questioning, however, give us an opportunity to hope, have faith, and choose to believe. Without doubt, we would have nothing to choose, for there must be grounds for doubt as well as belief, in order to render the choice more truly a choice."[5]

After choosing to have faith, to press forward, Francis said the price they paid to become acquainted with God was "a privilege to pay." Why would he say that suffering as much as he and the other Saints did was a privilege? Sometimes I wonder how suffering could be a privilege, something to be grateful for. But I've learned something about faith from Francis, and from my own experience. Choosing faith allows us to gain so much more than we could ever lose. I realized that the pains of life are a crucial refiner's fire, as spoken of in LDS Doctrine and Covenants (D&C), and "shall give thee experience, and shall be for thy good. The Son of Man hath descended below them all. Art thou greater than he?" (D&C 122:7-8). As we choose faith in the midst of trial, we become more like our Savior, who experienced every hardship, doubt, and loss we will experience. Although the loss is hard, it truly is a privilege to come closer to Christ, to truly be anchored in Him, and to be able to empathize with others and have compassion as He does because of the trials we have gone through. It is a privilege to gain that happiness, strength, and peace that comes through faith. These trials that give us the opportunity to choose to believe are truly for our good.

Even more so, it is a privilege to have trials, because as we do, as we choose faith in hard times and draw closer to our Savior, we are better able to recognize His hand, His love, and His tender mercies in our lives. And in a kind of positive feedback loop, or adaptive spiral, recognizing those tender mercies helps us continue to choose faith and helps our faith and our relationship with God increase.

One such tender mercy that came into my life was for Emi and me to receive a priesthood blessing at the hands of LDS President Thomas S. Monson. Only six months after my stroke, the stars aligned for this precious event when Emi and I, along with both sets of our parents, were visiting Nauvoo, Illinois, for the dedication of the rebuilt Nauvoo Temple. President Monson, who was close with my father and heard of my stroke, was very concerned about my wellbeing. When I first learned about the possibility of a meeting and that he might give me a blessing, I was a little hesitant, but I was grateful nonetheless to have the attention of a prophet of the Lord.

President Monson graciously invited us to his hotel room where he and his wife, Frances, had been staying. He shared with us precious details of their own personal lives, including that his dear Frances had been recently critically ill. Years before, the Monsons had come to our wedding. Now meeting with the Monsons, I noticed Sister Monson was indeed a little less interactive than I remembered her being at the wedding. I sensed President Monson was especially sensitive to the neurological injuries I was facing; however, he was hopeful and optimistic about our unique situation.

He took the time to give both Emi and me priesthood blessings. During each blessing, we could feel a measure of God's love and comfort flowing through President Monson, an inspired and righteous mouthpiece of the Lord. In my blessing, President Monson talked about the Lord being mindful of the little sparrows in the field, and how much more He is interested in our wellbeing as His children. President Monson was mindful of the challenges that lay before us, but he helped us to see the eternal perspective in a way that, perhaps, only he could. He made us feel like God was not only mindful of us, but He was indeed on our side to succor and champion our cause. He was in-tune with the spirit and told us exactly what we needed to hear. When we parted, I felt like all who witnessed the blessing—Emi, our parents, and me—had a clearer picture of the path set before us; each of us was strengthened and hopeful, and we felt joy in the road before us. I've also noticed smaller mercies in my life—meaningful conversation, acts of service—that have made a great impact on me and my family.

I've come to recognize that the Lord is inspiring others all around us to perform tender mercies. And He inspires us to do the same. Our trials give us experience so we might empathize with others and serve them. And as we both perform tender mercies and recognize them, our faith is strengthened. So often the seeds of faith start with an act of mercy by a fellow human being, and eventually, we recognize that God is the Source of that tender mercy, manifest on earth as love. Thus, our love for other people and of humanity grows…and faith grows.

In Victor Hugo's classic novel *Les Misérables* there is a story about Bishop Myriel, whose kindness provides a tender mercy to the story's protagonist Jean Valjean when Valjean hits rock bottom. After being released from prison, Jean Valjean is unable to find work. The bishop feeds him and gives him a bed—the first tender mercy we see in the story. However, Valjean does not recognize that tender mercy right away. Instead, Valjean seizes the opportunity by waking early and stealing the bishop's precious silver. He is caught by the police and would have been sent to the gallows, except that Bishop Myriel shows love and gives him his best silver, saying, "I am glad to see you. But! I gave you the candlesticks also, which are silver like the rest." By doing so, the good bishop raises Jean Valjean's soul out of the depth of hell and sends him toward a virtuous pathway, an adaptive spiral. The Bishop says, "Never forget that you have promised me to use this silver to become an honest man.... My brother, you no longer belong to evil, but to good. It is your soul that I am buying for you...and I give to God. Now, go in peace."[6] This was a second tender mercy from God to this poor man. Because the Bishop had chosen to believe in God and have faith, he was able to believe in God's love for Jean Valjean and be an instrument to provide mercy to him. Indeed, tender mercies by God's children are one of the manifestations of God's love for us.

Just as Bishop Myriel became an instrument for God's mercy and love, so, too, was Dr. Sheehan, a Jesuit priest and Dean of the Loyola School of Medicine in Chicago. He was an instrument of mercy and love to me by clearing my path back to a career in medicine. In the very early days after my stroke, he reminded me that I have a soul, and even though I may have felt lower than pond scum, he reminded me that God even clothes the lilies of the field. He acknowledged my suffering, and the suffering of the human condition, by weeping by my side. As Victor Hugo wrote in *Les Misérables*, "Surely, there is scarcely nothing but love in this world."[7] Father Sheehan, in a very real sense, became a Bishop Myriel figure in my life story. Father Sheehan bought my way back to medical residency by using his clout and influence. I am trying not to forget my promise to use this gift for the betterment of man and to honor God, and Father Sheehan set me toward a virtuous path.

Perhaps there comes into each of our lives inspired people who, by their tender mercy, raise us out of darkness and bring our souls closer to God. God worked a miracle, from a prophet's prayer, through a righteous and loving mortal man who heeded the inspired call. We must also realize that showing love to one another is essential to our lives with Christ, for our lives are, as Miller writes in *An Early Resurrection*, "not just with Christ, but with other people. It's impossible to be alive in Christ alone."[8] So often our faith starts with a tender mercy by another person, and we eventually recognize that God is the source of all goodness, causing our love for other people to grow.

I sometimes catch a glimpse of the wisdom and mercy of having difficult, sometimes painful experiences in this life. Though I walk by faith, sometimes in the dark, perhaps I am more understanding of people and their unique life stories because of the experiences and trials I have endured. The words of Rudyard Kipling in his poem "If" caused me to gain a deeper perspective and more courage when he said:

> If you can meet with Triumph and Disaster
> And treat those two impostors just the same....
> Yours is the Earth and everything that's in it,
> And—which is more—you'll then be a Man, my son.[9]

No matter whether we are facing dark times or light, we need to choose faith and recognize the tender mercies in our lives. I understand how, if I am spiritually in tune to recognize the tender mercies in my life and love others as Christ would have me love, this can lead me to be a more effective husband, father, and doctor. If we can choose faith, and hold it, our Heavenly Father will help us turn our struggles into triumphs. We will recognize tender mercies, and be an instrument to provide tender mercies to others.

CHAPTER 7

WHEN A DOOR CLOSES, MAKE A NEW ONE

It has often been said about life that "When a door closes, a window opens." However, sometimes in life, when that door closes, there are no windows, and we find ourselves in a very dark place. This is sometimes a result of the natural and imperfect world we live in. At those times, the power is often within us to do some remodeling on our own life situation, to choose to improve our circumstances, and to enable us to get back to our life journey. Although I don't believe God "causes" the misfortunes that befall us, I am reminded of a quote by C. S. Lewis that illustrates an important point:

> Imagine yourself as a living house. God comes in to rebuild that house. At first, perhaps, you can understand what He is doing. He is getting the drains right and stopping the leaks in the roof and so on; you knew that those jobs needed doing and so you are not surprised. But presently He starts knocking the house about in a way that hurts abominably and does not seem to make any sense. What on earth is He up to? The explanation is that He is building quite a different house from the one you thought of—throwing out a new wing here, putting on an extra floor there, running up towers, making courtyards. You thought you were being made into a decent little cottage: but He is building a palace. He intends to come and live in it Himself.[1]

With this in mind, I tried to view my own life, the new life I was trying to build, through these optics. It would require an aggressive, almost violent approach to rebuild my life from the dark desolation I felt. However, I had faith that a loving Heavenly Father would be my companion in the rebuilding process, guiding me in where to swing the sledge hammer and where to construct the new door. I began to feel what it means to live in Christ, even in this world, in this flesh. I had come so far, but given my stroke-related limitations, now I had to find a new path forward in medicine. I started to tell myself "When one door closes, tear down a wall and construct a new door."

The path I had chosen before my stroke was in the field of ophthalmology, a field dedicated to the medical and surgical care of the eye. I had secured my spot in that highly competitive field, and I was planning on completing my ophthalmology residency training in St. Louis after my intern year was complete. My stroke threw a wrench in my plan, but I still hoped to get to the program at St. Louis, though one year later. I was extremely disheartened when I learned that my residency spot was given away for the next year as well, meaning my one-year break from medicine would turn into a two-year break, if I still chose to go into ophthalmology. Furthermore, a trusted friend, with whom I counseled, told me, "maybe non-surgical ophthalmology is not the right field for someone in your unique situation." Hard as this was to hear—what seemed to be a clear indication of others' lack of confidence in me—these words sent me in a different, equally fulfilling direction. In my explorations for a specialty that would foster my interests as well as my abilities, I briefly considered cardiology, then radiation oncology. However, I seemed to be drawn back time and time again to the field responsible for my own recovery—physical medicine and rehabilitation. I acknowledge the Spirit's role in this decision, perhaps even letting the Savior steer the ship for a while. This decision has afforded countless blessings for me, my family, and my patients.

I returned to residency training to begin my journey to my current field on December 1, 2002, one year after my stroke, at Resurrection Hospital on the outskirts of Chicago. I had been a resident there, then a patient, and now I was a resident again. Many of the people I had worked with before were still there, and the setting was the same—it was as comfortable as residency training could be.

Just four days after my return, I was required to do my first overnight call, which meant being primarily responsible for the medical care of most of the hospital's patients. Although I had a more senior resident who would provide backup if needed, it was the custom not to bother the senior resident even though we would typically get bombarded with people being admitted to the hospital at night, with essentially only one resident to oversee their care.

Not knowing what the night ahead would entail and desperate to perform satisfactorily, I picked up two bottles of Mountain Dew, just in case I had to be up and working all night; I needed both. This was the beginning of a string of very long call nights. It became usual for me to have to work up, document, and write orders for six or seven new patients per night. We were required to call the attending physician at home to give a report on each patient after we completed the admission orders and got the patients settled in for the night. That first night, I called one physician and struggled through my speech impediment to give him a report at 1 a.m. After our conversation, the physician quickly called back to the floor nurse and asked, "Is this intern safe?" While he was skeptical of my abilities at first, he ended up being one of my biggest advocates.

I quickly realized that, by the nature of what I was, I forced people to have a strong impression of me, good or bad, immediately. I was under the microscope, much more than my peers, and I needed all the allies I could get. In time, I developed a good reputation as the intern who could keep complex patients, many of whom were on their last leg of life, alive overnight, until the morning handoff.

At the end-of-the-year graduation dinner, I was awarded "Most Outstanding Intern," but I knew this award had little to do with the actual care I had provided. This award by my colleagues represented their true compassion for and recognition of what I had gone through to return to medicine. Everyone wants something to believe in, someone to cheer for. I came to represent the underdog, the guy who was trying to make a comeback against all odds. Many people are drawn to a good story of redemption, which resonates within our hearts and minds. It seems our brains are wired to believe in something—perhaps that is what our Creator intended all along. As such, the award may have meant more to the people in the residency program than it did to me, for I knew I had miles to go before I could sleep—my job was not done.

I visited my very last patient during my internship a few days after graduation. I stayed for one last overnight on-call responsibility while Emi started moving our family back to Utah. When my beeper went off at 4 a.m., it showed a callback number I was very familiar with—the surgical floor.

A sixty-five-year-old man had pulled out his feeding tube. "We need you to come order a replacement," the floor nurse informed me. "Oh, by the way, his blood pressure is a little low, systolic of 90." The patient was unfamiliar to me. He was awake, but confused and mildly agitated. He didn't say much, though he looked like he wanted to say something. I wondered, *Can he not communicate? Is this his baseline cognitive function?* I went to the nurse's station for his chart and gave the order to replace his feeding tube, give him some intravenous fluids, and check a urinalysis. I also ordered some labs to be reviewed at morning rounds, about three hours away. When I asked the nurse about the patient's baseline functions, she told me, "This is my first time having him; I don't know much about what he's normally like." With no easy way of getting the information I wanted in the middle of the night (medicine is an imperfect science), and having seen dozens of patients confused at night like this before, I was satisfied that I had done my job and headed to the on-call room for a couple of hours of badly needed rest.

Unknown to me, an hour later, the code team was called for cardiac arrest and CPR was initiated on that very same man. The quiet scene I had encountered now became a critical fight to save a life, with multiple people running here and there, all attention on that one patient, who was going through the juggernaut. When CPR chest compressions are done properly, the violent compressions tend to crack the ribs. The family was called in. Seeing the blue-faced patient—a husband and father—being pounded on is hard for anyone to see, especially family members and loved ones. The patient's wife eventually told the medical staff to stop, and the man was pronounced dead.

I learned of this event early the next morning. I had some time to reflect, in the quiet of the on-call room that Saturday morning, before walking out the hospital doors for the last time. Perhaps that hospital was teaching me one final lesson.

Sooner or later, every doctor has to confront death, including the possibility that they played a role in a patient's decline. I asked myself hundreds of times, "Was I the cause? Was he trying to tell me something I ignored? Did I miss something?" On the grandest of stages—life or death—why didn't I sound the alarm or bring in the cavalry to save a stranger's life? I felt a sense of guilt for a life I couldn't save—wondering if I had missed something.

Some things we can never know for certain. Perhaps the "complete control" over life and death is a mirage we like to envision. I will never know the exact cause of this man's death. I will never know if I could have reversed his course. Even so, his case consumed my thoughts. I wrestled with the question of whether I could have saved this man and whether I was really ready to continue with my medical career. However, eventually I remembered God has a mechanism in place for such circumstances. They allow us to look back on what we've done, and either continue or correct our course. God knows us and knows our minds. Although we can't always know the "whys" and "hows" in life in all circumstances, we can have faith in His plan. In His love and wisdom, He has provided a way to unload our burdens, and a way to move on—called the Atonement of Jesus Christ. The Atonement of Christ isn't just for sinners; it's for all of us, for we all fall short.

LDS Apostle Dallin H. Oaks taught, "Apart from what we experience because of our sins, mortality is filled with frequent struggles, heartaches, and suffering.... Those who suffer [these] circumstances should remember that our Savior experienced this kind of pain also and that, through His Atonement, He offers the strength to bear it."[2] Book of Mormon prophet Alma explains this part of the Savior's Atonement as follows: "And he shall go forth, suffering pains and afflictions and temptations of every kind; and this that the word might be fulfilled which saith he will take upon him the pains and the sicknesses of his people (Alma 7:11). Oaks further explains that the "Savior has the power to succor—to help—every mortal pain and affliction. Sometimes His power heals an infirmity, but the scriptures and our experiences teach that sometimes He succors or helps by giving us the strength or patience to endure our infirmities."[3] The Savior knows what it feels like to face uncertainty in our careers and in every aspect of our lives. Because he felt the burdens of doubt I felt about my career, He can help us gain confidence as we move forward through our challenges.

Sometimes handing our burdens over to the Lord is the only way to move forward. With his strength and ability to carry our burdens and doubt, God can help us close the doors to past pain that torments us and guide us to healing, peace, and growth. Because the Savior both understands all that we go through and sees our potential for the future, He can give us strength to move on past difficult times and have faith in the future, even if we don't know all the answers to our doubts right now. We can trust in His grace and believe that one day we will see with full and perfect clarity as He does.

To some extent, we are all fumbling through life, with various missteps, while dealing with the traumas of life, human emotions, and human interactions—all while seeing with imperfect acuity. Tempered with the experience of my stroke, I could eventually see more clearly. The Atonement of Jesus Christ helps mend, relieve, and comfort so that we can move past difficult things like loss, illness, and even death. Faith in Christ's Atonement helps us gain a more eternal perspective, which has far-reaching effects, even infinite effects, in our lives. The Atonement is truly the linchpin that gives this life sense and meaning. Christ does this, as Fiona Givens insightfully and correctly articulates, by "not rescue[ing] us from a condition of original sin or depravity. Rather, He is primarily a healer of the wounds incident to a long-planned sojourn, one intended to immerse us in the trials, pains, and soul-stretching of this mortal schoolroom."[4]

I am indeed lucky to be married to Emi, a wonderful, strong, and courageous woman. In my darkest moments, Emi held on to the gospel treasure, with faith for the future, for both of us. When the world expected us to give up our dreams, Emi trusted in God's strength, in herself, and in the bond we had forged as a couple with a covenant God. In a real sense, Emi swung the sledgehammer. She did this by simply believing in me, and believing there were new unexplored territories for us to venture forward in, where we could blaze new paths and open new doors at those times when I was unable or unwilling to let go of the selfish parts of me. For I was, for a time, solely focused on getting back to the future that I thought eye surgery held for me. But I needed to be redeemed, here and now. I needed to let Christ take over. Emi helped me with this. For, together, "as Christ was raised up from the dead by the glory of the Father, even so *we* also should walk in *newness* of life. For if we have planted *together* in the likeness of his death we shall be also in the likeness of His resurrection" (Roman 6:4-5, emphasis added).

Going through adversity as a couple, although immensely helpful on the one hand, also presents some complexities, as both people separately try to make sense of and process the trial. Each has their own perspective; each wants to protect the other and themselves.

I believe we can learn from our first parents, Adam and Eve, and their eternal relationship. In the Garden of Eden, the door to have children was closed to Adam and Eve. I imagine Adam valued obedience and the protection provided by the Lord. Eve, on the other hand, valued growth and progress, and was willing to take a risk. Both people had valid and noble virtues. Both likely had their own separate and unique perspectives of their situation. It certainly took faith for Eve to take the first step; she may have been creating a new door when a path forward did not exist. That path forward enabled the plan of Salvation, in which God provided a Savior to come into the world, that through His grace, the whole of humankind would have the chance to be saved. They moved forward toward the future God had in store for them.

After Eve partook of the fruit, one of the biggest choices Adam had to make was whether they should separate or leave the Garden of Eden together. This lesson shouldn't go unnoticed. Both Adam and Eve had perspectives that, though different, were valid and of value. Both Adam and Eve saw the wisdom in the other's perspective; they stayed together and forged their way through life as a couple. Emi and I, as it is with all couples, can approach things from different angles and perspectives, and we are usually stronger by doing so. We can all approach issues with mutual love and respect, as our first parents did.

Indeed, we are each born with a set of preferences that are, by and large, maintained throughout life. Couples come together for a shared experience through marriage. That shared experience can be, in various aspects of the relationship, different in perspective. As such, we have different viewpoints in the family. We can begin to understand the intricate and somewhat delicate marriage relationship by looking to God. Paul wrote about this when he was referring to spiritual gifts that God gives. "The manifestation of the Spirit is given to every man [and woman] to profit withal. . . . For as the body is one, and hath many members, and all the member of that one body, being many, are one body: so also is Christ" (1 Corinthians 12: 7, 12). As Paul inferred about relationships, marriages that incorporate different perspectives don't represent weakness, but strength. Moreover, neither man nor woman become the head—Christ is the head of a consecrated marriage.

In the end, Adam and Eve chose to stay together, and that decision made all the difference.

I admit I can never truly walk in Emi's shoes or crawl into her brain. I believe I have a sacred obligation, however, to be understanding, empathetic, and compassionate. With a shared understanding of the eternal perspective, which the Savior's Atonement provides, Emi and I walk together and have faith in whatever the future holds for us. Emi has been an enormous blessing and benefit in my life; thanks be to God for sending her to me.

As I have moved forward through my medical training, I have had many experiences that challenged me and caused me to question my future. However, I have also have many experiences where doors were opened and I was able to work alongside my Heavenly Father to reach my goals. From all the experiences of my internship at Resurrection Hospital, I learned important lessons about mortality, that people die in spite of our best efforts, and about not second-guessing decisions, even when the stakes are high. I also learned about the healing power of Christ's Atonement, and the power Christ has to help us take steps toward the future He has in store for us.

By making it through my intern year, I had returned to a career in medicine, a major goal achieved, but more training and changes were still to come in our lives.

Toward the end of my intern year, I formally made a decision that would shape the remainder of my career—to pursue the field of physical medicine and rehabilitation. I interviewed at several top programs, including the Mayo Clinic, the University of Washington, and the University of Utah. I was eventually offered positions at all three, which meant Emi and I had a decision to make. On the one hand, the opportunity to study and work at places like the Mayo Clinic and the University of Washington were prestigious and exciting. However, I felt there was only so much we, both individually and as a couple, could endure. We had broad family support in Salt Lake City, which, at times, was much needed, so we chose the University of Utah's program.

Exciting doors opened for us even as others closed, reminding me again of C. S. Lewis's quote. Perhaps God is making a palace of our lives and guiding the things of utmost importance to us—family, education, career, and our highest aspirations—just not in the ways we had expected. Looking through the optics to recognize the palace being built around us requires faith in an eternal perspective to see the impact of Christ's Atonement in our lives. I choose to see that God has been with me throughout this journey.

CHAPTER 8

STAND, ACT, AND ENDURE TO THE END

In my extensive rehabilitation process, the desire to stand up and walk became a major driving force for me. Indeed, we are all highly motivated creatures when it comes to being able to stand and walk. We see this innate drive in infants, and also in adults who have suffered from strokes or spinal cord injuries. It is normal for people to take this ability for granted; only when this ability is taken away do we notice this yearning for strength to move as we please. Perhaps we can learn a lesson about mortal life from this inherent desire to stand.

Standing, in a sense, is more complex than just putting two feet beneath you and working your body upright. Rather, standing represents a choice first, and then an action, sometimes over and over, while enduring to the end. There are two aspects of what it means to stand up and act—standing up physically and standing up spiritually. Both forms of standing are intrinsically important. Perhaps the spiritual standing precedes the physical act, just as in a sense the spiritual creation precedes the physical creation. Nevertheless, the fortitude to make that choice to stand comes from a lifetime of experiences when we understand our emotions, our bodies, the natural world we live in, and the strength of the Lord to support us, especially in extreme circumstances.

When I was a thirteen-year-old boy at Scout camp, I had just such an experience—an experience that was extremely frightening, but formative for the rest of my life. This experience had an indelible effect on my character and illustrated for my young mind several complex and, at times, difficult facets of our life here on earth.

Camp Steiner was a scout camp at a 10,000-foot elevation in the Uintah Mountains. The grand culmination of the week, the capstone experience, was a literal rite of passage: a night camping with no adults to earn the Wilderness Survival merit badge. The requirements also limited our provisions to sleeping bags and some food, but no backpacks, tents, or tarps. The current requirements for the merit badge have not changed much, and they include, "show that you know first aid for hypothermia…frostbite, dehydration…avoid panic and maintain a high level of morale…describe the steps you would take to survive on cold, snowy, or wet conditions…improvise a natural shelter; spend a night in your shelter."[1] We had looked forward to this fun adventure to earn our mettle as we transitioned from boys to men.

When the appointed time arrived, we hiked the two or so miles into the steep, rugged mountains. There must have been more than thirty boys on this expedition, including the various scout troops at the camp and eight from my troop. All were boys, with no adults. We kept in mind the things taught to us in preparation for this one-night experience. The sole sixteen-year-old youth-leader led us up the trail for about thirty minutes. Then, with a fair amount of cautious apprehension, we divided into groups of four and disseminated around the rugged hills. We had no idea what we were in for.

Around 7 p.m., the skies grew dark and it began to rain. We had anticipated this possibility and prepared the best we could with our limited provisions. When the rain didn't stop and worry set in, we gathered together and one of the boys in the group offered a heartfelt prayer. Remarkably, it did stop raining, though briefly, but we were able to build a fire, cook, and eat our food. We quickly made a lean-to out of logs and branches from nearby towering pine trees, a shelter big enough for the four of us. We settled in to the lean-to for the night, trying to keep our sleeping bags dry, but the pine bough coverings just seemed to create a drippy, wet mess. At about 10 p.m. it started pouring rain, which we could handle. Then came the thunder. Lightning and thunderclaps came closer and closer, until we were enveloped in a highly dangerous, high-altitude lightning storm. With each lightning strike, we could feel the immense energy popping around us. To this day, I have never seen a thunderstorm like that with its frequency and proximity of lightning strikes. The lightning and thunder crashing all around us were deafening and frightening, and lasted at least a couple of hours. We knew people could die from lightning strikes! In fact, in our Wilderness Survival course, we had just learned that a common cause of death at scout camps is lightning strikes. We were terrified. Soon, our little group of four swelled to eight and then twelve, as other boys sought shelter in our makeshift lean-to designed for four. We were packed together like sardines in a wet and cold shelter, with emotions racing and no room to move. The temperature began to drop in the high elevation storm. Our now damp sleeping bags did little to guard us from the cold. Some of the boys began to shiver uncontrollably, have panic attacks, and even hallucinate. I knew then (as I know better now as a doctor) that they were experiencing the early stages of hypothermia. We took the boys having panic attacks outside to get them out of the very cramped space and try to calm them down. We prayed silently and earnestly. As the long night went on, I, too, began to shiver uncontrollably. I knew I was in serious danger of hypothermia from our training just a few days prior. We then made the decision for a life-saving measure—we took off most of our wet clothes and crawled into sleeping bags, two boys to a bag. We did what we had to do to survive, and that survival skill learned just days before likely saved us.

I know each one of us thought we were likely to die that night, either from the lightning or the cold. All any of us could do was hold on until the morning. We survived by keeping our emotions as calm as we could and doing what we could to protect and care for our bodies, despite nature's extreme conditions.

I awoke in the early morning light, surprised that I had been able to sleep…and that I was alive. The hard rain had stopped, and one by one, we crawled out of the cramped lean-to. We physically stood up for the first time in several hours. We were going to make it, thankfully.

As we hiked back to the main camp in somber silence, I felt grateful to be alive, but shell-shocked by nature's power. Now it began to snow, big snowflakes on a very cold August morning. We made it back and life moved on, and the sun rose on another day. We were greeted by our tremendously worried leaders; thankfully, no one had to go to the hospital.

This experience in the Uintahs became a defining moment in my young life. It gave me a healthy respect for the forces of the natural world—forces that men cannot control. I knew I could get through the harshest of nights, that I could stand up, both spiritually and physically.

For me, the lessons learned from this experience were profound. I realized the power is within me, whatever my circumstances, to choose my response to whatever life throws my way. To my young mind, in this case, high in a mountain storm, I thought this choice was a matter of life or death. Whatever the case, my life started to take shape. Armed with the knowledge of this power to choose, my confidence grew, and I could stand and act in any circumstance.

I was learning the lesson that undoubtedly God wants us all to learn—that we each have boundless potential, as a gift from Him, because of choice.

Since then, I have had other experiences, times in my life when God, it seems, chose not to intervene against the forces of nature. During such times, we have to stand and act. For me, those times have been some of the hardest to endure, but they have also been when I have learned the most about standing up on the inside.

We can all stand up on the inside spiritually…before the physical act of standing is possible. Through our own unique life experiences, we understand our emotions and our bodies and minds, and we find strength in the Lord, in spite of the natural world we live in. We can set a pattern of choosing our response, then acting on that choice, then enduring to the end. For me, that pattern started in my youth and has come to represent the term standing up on the inside.

As a young boy at scout camp trying to get through the dark and stormy night, my young mind wondered why our repeated pleas to our Heavenly Father didn't stop the storm once and for all. *The tempest is raging; please, please calm the storm*, I pled over and over again. But nature can be harsh, and sometimes all you can do is hold on, gathering strength in the hope to be able to stand up and act once again. Similarly, LDS leader John H. Groberg wrote about his harrowing mission experience in Tonga. He almost drowned when his small boat was overturned in a violent squall. Groberg points out that even though the Lord has the power to calm the storms in our lives, and sometimes He does, more often "He lets the storm rage on…and calms His child."[2]

In His wisdom, He quiets the turmoil that rages inside us and helps us build the courage and fortitude to stand up on the inside and work ourselves out of perilous situations.

Much later, I learned that the key to this process of spiritually choosing to stand and act requires an act of faith. We have that choice because of a gift unique to the human family—we have the ability to choose our responses, and then act. This ability to choose was a gift to Adam and Eve from God, and from God to each of us.

In our Heavenly Father's Plan of Happiness, a few events were critical to allow mortal beings to have the ability and the choice to stand up and act in this fallen world, including the creation of earth, the creation of life, and the creation of man. Our Heavenly Father offered us a choice in the pre-mortal existence to come to earth and experience joy as well as pain; then He placed a veil over our minds, even that of primitive man. We know we had the power to choose in the pre-mortal existence, but perhaps that ability was regifted to us in this life. God's creation of what we call "man" may not have been complete until God breathed into Adam the "breath of life," as spoken of in Genesis 2:7. It may be that the "breath of life" was God's gift of consciousness, the self-awareness that was necessary for the first man and woman here on earth.

In fact, Michelangelo depicted this monumental scene on the Sistine Chapel's ceiling in 1512. Today, art and science scholars debate whether in the scene God and His cherubim are intentionally wrapped in a cloak shaped in the form of a human brain and brainstem.[3] Given Michelangelo's detailed knowledge of anatomy, although constrained by social norms of the time, it could be that Michelangelo covertly captured the moment in art when God bestowed consciousness, represented in God's finger touching Adam's.

Consciousness, at its core, allowed choice and agency to be present in our lives. Because of the veil that was placed over our minds, choice permits God's sons and daughters the option to stand up and act.

For centuries, the concept of consciousness has perplexed philosophers and scientists. We have yet to find any specific location in our brains responsible for consciousness. Scientifically, we use the word consciousness to refer to our ability to be self-aware, be sentient, or have the ability to feel empathy. Others define consciousness as the sum of the conscious experiences we have, such as thoughts, emotions, and sensations. However, in looking for evidence of consciousness, all we can find are the certain behaviors we think are closely related with conscious experience—attention, self-awareness, access to information, and the ability to comprehend and communicate.

This consciousness has enabled self-awareness of our decisions from the time of Adam to the present day. Since Adam and Eve partook of the fruit, we have had the moral sense of right and wrong. Consciousness is the engine that our moral sense runs on, and it allows and permits our day-to-day choices, from routine tasks to decisions that may have eternal consequences. In this way, we are all free to choose our responses—large and small—to the barrage of provocations and incitements we encounter every day.

I feel I may have special insight into this concept of consciousness because, during the first hours after my stroke, I was stripped down to a state of simple consciousness—nothing else. In that state, I was unable to move, speak, or communicate effectively—things we typically think define what it is to be human. In the absence of these basic faculties, the physical entity that remained with my body was still me because I could still think, could form memories, was aware, and could comprehend my situation. Most of us probably fail to appreciate fully this singularly remarkable gift, aptly called the breath of life, which enables agency and choice. Our choice is to be spiritually strong and stand up on the inside before we do so physically.

When our first daughter, Eliza, was stillborn, Emi and I had the difficult choice of how to respond to that heart-wrenching situation. During Emi's pregnancy, she and I would lay on the bed at night and take turns listening to the baby's tiny heartbeat through my newly acquired stethoscope (I was in my second year of medical school). One night, Emi asked me to listen again because she hadn't felt the baby kicking for several hours. I listened for several minutes, trying and hoping to hear something. But I couldn't hear that tiny heart beating.

We decided we should call the hospital. The OB nurse tried to reassure us over the phone, but told us to come in right away. At the hospital, the doctor confirmed our worst fears—our baby had died with just six weeks left of gestation. Our hearts were broken wide open. Our mortal, human minds and hearts could not comprehend this loss; we still struggle to understand how this happened.

Eliza was our first child, perfect in every way, but lifeless. We held her close for as long as we could before the medical staff had to take her sweet body away. Those were precious moments—though she had died, we felt her spirit close. We yearned to live, if only for a moment, in either one of the two gardens, just not in this harsh world, a world where sometimes babies die before even taking their first breath of air. Still, our place was in the space between the two gardens. In those excruciatingly painful and difficult hours, our hopes and dreams of raising this beautiful child were crushed.

I struggled to understand why this had happened—why it had happened to us. My pain turned to tears, and occasionally to sobbing, for what seemed like hours at the hospital. In anguish, I asked myself, "Why was I not able to protect Emi from this tragic loss?" It was as if we were on a lifeboat with no oars, bobbing around, at the mercy of the mighty sea.

Upon release from the hospital, Emi and I were shocked and amazed that people were just living their everyday lives, totally unaware of the trauma we had experienced. We were aware that life moves on. The sun still rises. But, with time, we realized we had to move on; we had to stand and act, despite how difficult it might be. Christ extended a loving hand to help us, and we chose faith to stand up on the inside, act, and move.

Yet again, a few years later, it was tempting to feel like all was permanently lost when my body completely failed me during my devastating stroke. By this point, I was getting quite used to being knocked down from traumatic events. Each time, while trying to cope with the loss, I wondered if it was truly a blessing to still be alive. I wondered what kind of life I was capable of living, given the traumatic, harsh events. Each time, it was necessary to have faith, to stand up on the inside before being able to act and move on. With each time, perhaps, I realized more firmly that the Savior's strength and love are sufficient, and His extended, loving hand helped me fully stand up on the inside, supporting me to endure to the end.

LDS leader Gary B. Sabin related the story of a young boy on a long-awaited trip to the toy store. The boy was fascinated by the abundance of objects, but he gravitated to one particular toy—a blow-up punching dummy that seemed magically to stand up whenever it was knocked down. No matter how hard or how many times it was knocked down, it always self-righted. This captivated boy's father asked him, "Why do you suppose the punching bag always stands right up again?" The boy simply replied, "I guess he's standing up on the inside."[4] Often, maybe most of the time, we have to dig within our own soul and character first to learn how to stand up on the inside, before we can physically stand, then repeat it, sometimes over and over—enduring to the end.

In each situation, good or bad, we are safe in His arms, and have experiences firsthand with His saving grace, which gives us courage and strength. We learn lessons from the storms of life that we cannot learn when the skies are calm. Whether we are twelve boys huddled in a lean-to in a mountain storm or a young couple dealing with the loss of a newborn far away from home, God can find us, succor us, and give us the courage to survive.

However, sometimes our human minds think if we do things in a certain way—are faithful and keep the commandments—certain results should follow. But God has placed us in this natural world, between two gardens, to sometimes experience traumatic and cruel storms. We need to leave the reasons for the storms—including this sometimes harsh world we live in with our mortal bodies, and with natural consequences—leave those things with the Lord, and work to overcome the challenges placed before us.

In his book *The Uses of Adversity*, Carlfred Broderick said, "The gospel of Jesus Christ is not an insurance plan against pain. It is a resource in the event of pain, and when that pain comes (and it will come because we came here on earth to have pain among other things), when it comes, rejoice that you have resource to deal with your pain."[5] We will all experience pain and struggles—it's part of life. We know that health problems and accidents are a natural part of life.

Since the time of Adam and Eve, we have had to walk by faith. We are required to develop faith in the Lord's Plan of Happiness in order to reap the benefits and assurances that plan provides. We have the ability to choose our response and stand up on the inside for truth and right—and endure to the end.

In the LDS faith tradition, we believe we all enthusiastically volunteered for this experience in the pre-mortal existence. We knew that perilous things like lightning strikes, strokes, accidents, and even untimely death would be part of life, although we may not have fully comprehended the pain and sorrow they would bring. I imagine we carefully weighed our options, and eventually chose to come to earth. We knew the risks. I imagine most of us were very solemn about this great opportunity, but there also must have been some trepidation for what we were about to experience—the loss, the pain, and the separation. But perhaps if we could see more than we see through mortal eyes, we would see that it was all worth it; that it was truly the only way, because a "Savior" would be provided, that we could learn and grow, and that we could be reunited with Divinity after this "brief" sojourn. We knew it was a risk—a risk of having hardships, but a risk worth taking. We knew it was the only way to progress and be nurtured, sometimes in quiet, but always in loving ways. It was the only way to become like our Heavenly Father and the Savior and receive exaltation.

Thus, our first parents left the garden with the aptitude and intuition to reason between right and wrong, gain intelligence, cooperate, and express and receive love. We also experience sorrow and pain, along with joy and happiness. It's quite possible, as John Milton suggested in the fictional story *Paradise Lost* in 1667, that Adam and Eve found "paradise within thee, happier far"—experiencing a form of happiness, in a different way, out of the Garden, compared to when they were in the state of pure innocence in the Garden.[6]

The relationship between Adam and Eve and God changed when Adam and Eve left the Garden of Eden, with God now becoming an unseen omnipresent being, except for the whisperings of the Spirit. Nevertheless, the whole human family can experience "joy," as spoken by Book of Mormon prophet Nephi, "Adam fell that man may be, men are, that might have joy" (2 Nephi 2:25).

In each of our lives, and with each traumatic event we go through in this life, though sometimes we cannot see from one day to the next, faith can play a critical and helpful role. For, as Paul said to the Philippians, "I can do all things through Christ which strengtheneth me" (Philippians 4:13). Though sometimes shell-shocked from the experiences, and though our lives are completely changed from many experiences we will each have in this life, the sun still rises each day, and we must still go on. With the Savior's help, we can fully stand up on the inside, and endure to the end, to the point where bitter things can have a sweetness about them.

I now count the knowledge that there is a plan and a purpose for our sorrows and suffering as one of my most precious blessings. God watches over us. And although He could intervene every time a bad or painful experience is about to occur, doing so would thwart His plan for our progress. God does not cause bad things to happen. He allows challenges in each of our lives because it's one of the ways we grow. In this way, our lives can be, should be, an ascent, and we can rise. The real work of our lives is defined by falling, which we all will do, and then learning to get back up. It is facing challenges and then learning how to overcome them—stumbling, but still finishing the race. Understanding this concept, though it often takes tremendous amounts of faith, enables us to have purpose in all the events of life, especially the most challenging ones.

Perhaps we will eventually see that, as sure as the sun rises—and the Son riseth, His strength and love are sufficient, even at the times when we thought we couldn't go on. We can stand up and act in faith, and endure to the end. Whether the "end" is the morning after a stormy and cold night or the end to our own mortal experience, we are charged with the responsibility to endure to the end. Perhaps we will yet praise His name for things we don't completely understand and for the sorrows that lay quietly within our hearts, as we struggle to find hope, between two gardens.

CHAPTER 9

THE HUMAN CAPACITY FOR HAPPINESS: A NEUROLOGICAL AND SPIRITUAL PERSPECTIVE

I love skiing. Although I am not as good as I was before my stroke, I absolutely love the cool, crisp mountain air, and with each turn on my skis, I get a little rush. Using only one ski pole to accommodate for my stroke-weakened right side, my right ski acting more like a rudder on a boat, my strong left side and my two strong hips do the work of carving turns and navigating myself down the mountain. Sailing on two skis, through the natural beauty of the mountains and forests in the winter—not too fast to be out of control—I feel free and unencumbered by this life's trivial concerns. While I love to ski with a companion, I also love the solitary skiing experience as I work, and turn, and glide down the mountain. For me, the skiing experience is more valued, even treasured, because of the work, effort, and hopes fulfilled to get on the mountain again, after my stroke made it seem this type of activity and level of freedom would be impossible—a pipe dream. Like Henry David Thoreau a couple of centuries ago, I go to the mountains "to live deep and suck the marrow of life."[1] Being outdoors now brings a measure of independence; often you don't value a thing until it's taken away for a time. Maybe it's not the highest form of happiness, maybe it won't lead to exaltation, but it puts my mind into the proper frame to appreciate and contemplate this life God has given me, and the loving relationships in it. It refreshes my spirit. It makes me thankful for the blessings in my life. And, as has been said, it may not add years to my life, but it adds life to my years.

This chapter is about the human capacity for happiness, and our brain's role in this emotion. The "pursuit of happiness" is woven into the fabric of the American Dream, yet so often, the happiness we pursue evades us. Happiness appears to be important to all peoples and societies, and also central to our Heavenly Father's plan for His children.

Cultivating true happiness—happiness that touches us so we can achieve a higher quality of life—is a goal many people seek. However, it's often a mistake to pursue materialism and status as the way to true happiness. "Most of the luxuries and many of the so-called comforts of life are not only not indispensable, but positive hindrances to the elevation of mankind," remarked Henry David Thoreau.[2] Happiness is not about having possessions—it's much simpler, and, for most of us, the key to happiness is hardwired within our brains.

God has given most of us the tools to achieve happiness; however, these tools are not what most people would instinctively think. The Creator formed our minds, from a neurological standpoint, to experience happiness as simply a result of our brain detecting the changes of dopamine. Dopamine is released between neurons in brief bursts of electrical activity—this is how neurons communicate with each other. When dopamine levels increase, we experience the sensation we call happiness. On the other hand, our brain must know what it's like to have no dopamine—a "baseline"—which leads to the experience of sorrow and depression.

However, this dopamine model is an oversimplification of the brain's inner workings, which are still being studied. Regardless, the concept and point is the same: Our brains are designed to experience both sorrow and happiness, and one cannot exist without the other.

In the Book of Mormon, Lehi explains the human mind's capacity to recognize these opposites:

> For it must needs be, that there is an opposition in all things. If not so...righteousness could not be brought to pass, neither wickedness, neither holiness nor misery, neither good nor bad. Wherefore, all things must needs be a compound in one; wherefore, if it should be one body it must needs remain dead, having no... happiness nor misery. (2 Nephi 2:11)

Often, true happiness comes from experiencing profound loss. From both a religious and scientific context, happiness and sorrow exist so we can appreciate and comprehend the magnitude of the blessings we normally enjoy. Dr. Richard Davidson, founder of the Center for Healthy Minds, describes happiness as "the capacity to remain upbeat and to sustain positive emotion over time." He explains that there is no such thing as pleasure without pain.[3]

Furthermore, we can and do make changes in our brains on a daily basis, including in our capacity to appreciate and experience happiness. Dr. Davidson says, "We can take most responsibility for our own brains, and shape our brains wittingly in a more intentional way by cultivating healthy habits of the mind."[4]

A 2013 study in the scientific literature shows the brain's ability to change in respect to "altruism." Altruism is the belief in or practice of selfless concern for others' wellbeing. This study found that "compassion can be cultivated with training and that greater altruistic behavior may emerge from increased engagement of neural [brain] systems implicated in understanding the suffering of other people, executive and emotional control, and reward processing."[5]

Altruism has another name in Christian culture: charity, the pure love of Christ. In other words, we have scientific evidence that we can physically change our brains through intentional effort to develop and cultivate charity. The Savior taught that "He that findeth his life shall lose it; and he that loseth his life for my sake shall find it" (Matthew 10:39). Christ is teaching us that if you want to find yourself, you've got to be willing to lose yourself first.

Our ability to gain true and lasting happiness stems from our ability to build loving relationships with others. As humans, we yearn for social and loving connections. As Nephi explains, this love is "the most desirable above all things...and the most joyous to the soul" (1 Nephi 11:22-23). Participation and engagement in churches that teach these altruistic principles help us internalize and obtain true joy and happiness; the closer we are bound up to Christ, the closer we are to love and the resultant happiness.

When a person goes through a trial, the depths of a person's agony may actually enable that person, at other times, to appreciate joy and happiness. The writer Henry Dreher explains, "Research has shown that our health is protected when we express a full range of emotions, including the so-called negative ones. When we find constructive ways to express, anger, grief and fear, we prevent lapses into, hopelessness, depression and passivity.... Unless we explore and express these primary human emotions, we cannot receive the information they carry."[6] The human mind and brain is surprisingly resilient. Human beings not only overcome difficult events quickly, but we generally rise above the difficulty, and come out of adversity as happier people.[7]

In my medical practice, I sometimes share with patients how even when their physical loss is great, a stroke provides an opportunity for great spiritual growth that may be able to offset that painful loss. Overcoming trials and the new perspective learned after any significant challenge can bring a sense of accomplishment and joy. After all, God has a keen interest in our growth and our ability to rise and ascend; He is author of all joy.

We have evidence that God has these same emotions, just on a much grander scale. Why else would He "weep" in sorrow, as Enoch attests in the Book of Moses (Moses 7:28-40)? Terryl and Fiona Givens explain, "If God, like us, is susceptible to immense pain, He has, like us, the greater capacity for happiness. The presence of such pain serves the larger purpose of God's master plan, which is to maximize the human capacity for joy.... God does not instigate pain and suffering, but He can weave it into His purposes." Furthermore, they suggest that God's power, at least partially, is in His "ability to alchemize suffering, tragedy, and loss into wisdom, understanding, and joy."[8] To have sorrow about events in your own life and the lives of those you love is a godly characteristic, leading to the ability to obtain even greater joy.

We often confuse happiness with fun. Our human brains are wired for long-term enjoyment and some brains are wired also for short-term pleasure. Long-term enjoyment is typically what we refer to as happiness, while short-term pleasure can be referred to as fun. Fun is transient enjoyment, amusement, or lighthearted pleasure. Fun is regulated in the brain as small bursts of dopamine in brain areas responsible for reward. These small bursts bring enjoyment to your day and have importance to the individual, such as creating a sense of satisfaction for a job well-done, getting a strike when bowling, or the thrill of gliding down a snowy slope on skis, for example. Fun is certainly a component to happiness, but true happiness is something much deeper.

Happiness is built on the foundation of deeper emotions like an appreciation of the life you have, the positive connections you have built with others, and the achievements that give you a sense of personal pride. One main purpose of our mortal experience is to experience joy and happiness. Many people perceive fun as happiness; however, as Helen Keller explains, "Happiness is not attained through self-gratification, but through fidelity to a higher purpose."[9] Lasting happiness hinges on our ability to build loving relationships with others...and with Christ. In the end, loving relationships are the only thing that brings lasting joy.

In God's love and mercy, He has "wired" us to respond to the simplest of things, that we may be happy. The dopamine response when we perform altruistic acts creates in our brains an upward spiral, or a virtuous cycle, where doing more good becomes easier and more rewarding.

We are also prone to be deceived, modulated by the same dopamine response, when one bad decision is rewarded by a burst of dopamine that leads to another bad decision, and another. Pornography and other addictive behaviors, while at first they may seem fun, lead to changes in the brain by this same process. Ceaseless obsession with social media causes similar dopamine responses. While these examples may seem harmless to some and "fun," they are really subtly and silently changing the brain—changing how the neurons "synapse," the strength of connections within our brains, and ultimately, the behavior of that individual.

Because of our affinity to be tempted into wrong choices, even subtly and subconsciously, it's no wonder the poet John Keats described this life as, "straining at particles of light in the midst of a great darkness."[10] We undoubtedly "see through a glass, darkly" as the apostle Paul writes. Perhaps this is what Nephi envisioned for our day as the "flaxen cords" that bind our brains, then bind our actions, and lead us away from the true happiness the gospel provides and feeling the love of God (2 Nephi 26:22). We read, "Let virtue garnish thy thoughts unceasingly; then shall thy confidence wax strong in the presence of God; and the doctrines of the priesthood shall distil upon thy soul as the dews from heaven" (D&C 121:45). Our Heavenly Father has given us the Spirit that speaks to our minds, as the dews from the Heavens, to even change the character of our minds, as we choose to draw close to Him and His love.

Because we are human, we are limited, as God intended, in our understanding of His plan for us. These limitations can and commonly do affect our interactions and relationships with others and, likewise, with our Heavenly Father. Jesus Christ, in His short mortal ministry, clarified God's desires for all of his children in the simplest of terms, now known as the "Two Great Commandments." Christ taught, "Thou shalt love the Lord thy God with all thy heart, and with all thy soul, and with all thy mind.... And the second is like unto it, Thou shalt love thy neighbor as thyself. On these two commandments hang all the law and the prophets" (Matthew 22:37, 39-40).

We know God has a great interest in how we treat ourselves and our neighbors. Our deliberate actions matter. They matter in how we take care of ourselves and others. We all struggle sometimes with keeping the subconscious mind and automatic behaviors in check. We have all struggled with kicking a bad habit, even one so benign as chewing our fingernails or excessive fidgeting.

After my stroke, however, I realized how much those automatic behaviors assist in our everyday lives. Struggling to relearn to walk and especially to speak, things that mostly occur outside the realm of conscious thought, was a daily challenge. That I had to think intently about every syllable and word, the placement of the tongue and lips, to form speech, taught me how much the subconscious mind does for us. One friend commented years after the stroke that I don't really have to worry about saying "idle words" or having something just slip out of my mouth—everything I say is said with added intentional effort.

In essence, all of the basic things we are encouraged to do—church attendance, scripture study, prayer, temple attendance—assist us in aligning our subconscious and automatic behaviors to allow us to be receptive to the Spirit's whispering.

On our journey toward exaltation, which is God's utmost desire for us (Moses 1:39), we can more intently and deliberately do two things to draw nearer to God. First, we are taught that "The natural man receiveth not the things of the Spirit" (1 Corinthians 2:14). This means we must act deliberately to suppress the natural man and not be swayed by the whims of our impulses and our adverse automatic behaviors; these include biases and unhealthy habits, to name a couple. This ability to control our impulses is a learned skill.

When the brain is injured or altered, it adds another layer of complexity to an already complex situation of dealing with day-to-day life and its accompanying emotions, demands, and stresses. Working with patients offers me a unique window into the ways our brains, injured or healthy, affect actions and behavior.

I believe God created us to be generally moral and good. We have evidence of this intent in both a religious and scientific context. Richard Davidson explains, "There are a number of…strong empirical findings which are consistent in showing that we indeed come into the world with this quality of innate basic goodness. What we're doing is nurturing seeds which are already present."[11] We believe the Light of Christ is an influence for good in the lives of all people; "And the Spirit giveth light to every man that cometh into the world" (D&C 84:46). We are born with an innate goodness, to differing extents, and most have the strong ability to love. But that goodness can also be learned and strengthened.

Nonetheless, when something like a stroke or other brain injury occurs, it can impair specific, discreet functions of the brain. There are just as many ways the brain can malfunction as there are actual functions of the brain. It is useful to contemplate these extremes in brain function to learn more about ourselves.

One devastating, but also interesting, stroke syndrome happens when damage occurs to the junction between the right frontal, parietal, and temporal lobes. This junction houses the centers largely responsible for judgment, intentional goal-oriented behavior, insight and self-awareness, and impulse control. This understanding has led some within the field of neuroscience to call this area the brain's "governing center." Damage to this area can cause dangerous changes in behavior due to a lack of impulse control and judgment, sometimes leading to a person harming self and others. It can disrupt or diminish a person's capacity to resist addiction, avoid injury, and avoid sin. In other words, the brain can inhibit a person from "putting off" the natural man and yielding to the Spirit's promptings.

To illustrate this undesirable behavior, let's look at an example of how it manifests itself. One of my patients whom I'll call Jen was a thirty-six-year-old mother who became addicted to heroin years ago. Her intravenous drug use caused an infection on her heart valve. The infection caused a clot to form that went up to her brain and caused a small stroke. Unfortunately, this stroke was exactly in the worst place in her brain: her governing center. Her stroke led to an alarming pattern of behavior defined by her lack of judgment, inappropriate comments, and a fixation on getting drugs to shoot through her accessible intravenous line, which we needed to use for her antibiotics. She referred to her IV line as a constant trigger due to it providing her with easy access to shoot up.

To find a solution to the problems this behavior was causing, we had a medical team and family conference, which Jen attended. In our conference, I saw two distressed parents who obviously loved their daughter but had already been through a lot on Jen's behalf. Jen, on the other hand, was placid and docile throughout the conference, with no evident ill intent or malice. She talked of wanting to inject heroin into her IV line just as casually and benignly as if she were asking for a drink of water. She said this many times, fixating on that one thought, even though IV drug use was what got her into this situation in the first place. She didn't have the cognitive understanding that if she did what she wanted, she could die. A four-year-old with a bottle of bubblegum-flavored poison would have been safer to herself. Her stroke knocked out the governing center that controls her insight into her situation and her ability to make a rational decision—she seemed to have no concept that her actions would have dire consequences. It would be wrong to discount her prior pattern of behavior in leading to this difficult situation, but, clearly, the stroke affected her judgment, her impulse control, and her ability to make rational decisions. Any filters she had previously possessed were now significantly diminished, if not completely shut off. It's as if all her subconscious thoughts and patterns now had access to the surface—if she had an inappropriate thought, she expressed it; if she had an impulse, she acted on it.

Somehow, with the stroke-induced brain damage, a large measure of her free will had been taken away. She no longer had the capacity to filter her unconscious thoughts or rationally think through the consequences of her actions. If free will can be limited with something as fairly commonplace as a stroke in the right location, it poses a question about the nature of free will. It also raises deep questions about personal responsibility and judging and regulating ourselves. Is the actual amount of free will we have an illusion—something we tell ourselves we have so we can feel more "in control" of our lives? Is most of what we do somehow genetically and environmentally predetermined? So much happens in our subconscious brain that is beneath the bright light of conscious thought: impulses, some of which may be protective yet also can be self-destructive, habits that are difficult to break, as well as biases that affect our actions and behaviors. We can't ignore that we have a subconscious brain, an unseen brain, out of conscious view.

Essentially, we have two brains, a conscious and a subconscious one, tethered together. Normally, these two brains act fairly synergistically. We typically have "veto" power over the subconscious mind allowing us to self-censor both our behaviors and speech, thereby suppressing unconscious drives and behaviors. But the bright circle of conscious thought becomes narrower when we think about what we actually and deliberately decide to do.

For example, many can't seem to see the personal dangers of prescription pain medications, which have given rise to the current opioid epidemic. Additionally, our minds are misled through social media, where we often compare ourselves with other people's perfectly curated best selves, or even their fake selves. Frequently, depression ensues. Whatever the case, these deceptions lead to a change in our focus and behavior, and, with time, they produce actual changes in how our minds function. It would seem our minds are wired in such a way that we need to be cautious about being misled. Sometimes, this misleading is benign, yet other times it provides the stimulus for dire consequences. All this conscious and subconscious brain activity influences, if not determines, happiness.

It's also easy to judge yourself when your subconscious mind delivers unattractive and unappealing messages about the person you are, your role here on earth, and your divine relationship with God. Too often, people feel like they are not measuring up to a certain standard and engage in persistent self-criticisms. This is not the spirit of peace whispering to us, nor the way to happiness. Though the devil cannot control our thoughts, as the Father of Lies, he can perpetuate falsehoods by persuasion, for he knows the base human emotions of fear and pain, and how to manipulate our subconscious minds into his perverse ways. We can begin to overcome these invasive thoughts, as the Book of Mormon teaches, by "yield[ing] to the enticings of the Holy Spirit, and put[ing] off the natural man and becom[ing] a saint through the atonement of Christ" (Mosiah 3:19).

Perhaps we need to be a little easier on ourselves and on others. To take more deep breaths in our labors and interactions during our travails between the two gardens. To realize no one is perfect, and we also cannot expect perfection in ourselves. We can focus on the journey and on the process of improvement. Recognizing improvement in our performance and behaviors is one way to gain happiness.

What we intentionally do (our actions and behaviors) becomes a much smaller component than what we think or perceive (our impulses, drives, and base emotions). Nevertheless, we are all, at least partially, governed by automatic behaviors. But we also bear personal responsibility for our actions; this personal responsibility is central to God's plan.

In my faith tradition, we believe we lived as spirits before we were born in mortality, but a veil was placed over our minds separating what we can remember from this mortal life and our lives before coming to earth. Perhaps there is yet another veil to our minds—the one between conscious and unconscious thought—purposefully placed, by design, by our Creator. I feel it is the Spirit, the Holy Ghost, who can help us peel back the veil between conscious and unconscious thought to see things more clearly; this, in turn, affects our ability to make good choices that lead to happiness.

It is difficult to affect a thought that does not even make it to the bright circle of consciousness. I believe LDS President Ezra Taft Benson taught a valuable lesson about keeping our subconscious biases and thoughts in check when he said, "The Lord [through the voice of the Spirit] works from the inside out. The world works from the outside in. The world would take people out of the slums. Christ would take the slums out of people, and then they would take themselves out of the slums. The world would mold men by changing their environment. Christ changes men, who then change their environment. The world would shape human behavior, but Christ can change human nature."[12] Christ's teachings and the Spirit's influence can help peel back the veil and affect our ability to make good choices that lead to happiness.

Perhaps the best guide to happiness in our behavior is imagining what Christ would do and, as much as possible, praying to be more fully able to follow His example. Although my stroke did not cause the type of damage Jen had, the practice of imagining what Christ would do made a difference in my recovery. I wanted and needed both the conscious and subconscious parts of my brain to be acting in concert for my recovery. I prayed for the spirit to peel back the veil so I could act in ways that would eventually lead to true happiness. Among other things, I tried to meld my mind to the right frame by reciting one of the most powerful and relevant prayers I have encountered. Each day, in the weeks leading up to restarting my residency program and during the first few months of that program, as I stated earlier, I pled to the Lord, using St. Francis of Assisi's prayer: "Lord, make me an instrument of Thy peace. Where there is hatred, let me sow love; where there is injury, pardon; where there is doubt, faith; where there is despair, hope; where there is darkness, light; where there is sadness, joy.... [G] rant that I may not so much seek to be consoled as to console."[13]

I thought of this prayer throughout those long days. I thought of Christ, His example, and what He has already done for me, of His love. This gave me a sense of shared hope for the future. I believe it made a difference in getting my mind "right" and aligning my conscious and subconscious thoughts and actions; eventually, it increased happiness within my life.

True happiness is the Savior's to give—it equates to love. Paul was pretty straightforward when he explained this. He said:

> If I speak in the tongues of men or of angels, but do not have love, I am only a resounding gong or a clanging cymbal. If I have the gift of prophecy, and can fathom all mysteries and all knowledge; and if I have a faith that can move mountains, but do not have love, I am nothing.... Love never fails. But where there are prophecies, they will cease; where there are tongues, they will be stilled; where there is knowledge, it will pass away. (1 Corinthians 13:1-2, 8 NIV)

Love is likely happiness in its truest form.

Everything will fail in this life, except for love. This means when talents, money, prestige, desires, and goals all fail, we will see that all we ever have needed is love. This means we cannot anticipate future happiness by achieving anything except for love. All of these false idols—

the big house, the expensive car, the fancy clothes, and other worldly desires—will pass away before we, ourselves, pass away…and we are left with love. Perhaps this is why loving relationships are so important to God and important to our human minds. This is also why so much emphasis is on family relationships—eternal relationships.

The brain feeds the human organism what it has been conditioned to provide for our primitive survival. These shallow things—our impulses, drives, and base emotions—might bring a burst of dopamine to our brains, but they will not bring lasting joy and happiness. What Christ teaches is to foster loving relationships, and that's exactly what the scientific research shows ultimately brings us happiness.[14]

Love is a very powerful motivating factor. Love between husband and wife. Love between father and daughter. Personally, I did a great many hard things in my recovery out of hope for the love of a baby girl, Ella Jayne, who was just nine months old when her daddy had a massive stroke. I hoped to raise her to the light—in righteousness and happiness. Hope for this love, and our Heavenly Father's love, sustained me.

When Ella was growing past the toddler age, Emi and I desired to have another baby. This desire, at its core, is a hope and promise of love for another human being that we can care for and nurture. By the gift of God, our baby, Louisa Kate, was born in early 2005. The first time I held Louisa in the newborn nursery, I experienced a joy for which there are no words to explain. Yet I found myself regretting the things I knew I wouldn't physically be able to do for and with her. In a world where I cannot control many of her life events, and all these things will pass away regardless, all I could do is pledge my time, undying love, support, and protection to the infant in my arms. Love is what I can offer my family. Perhaps this love is what Helen Keller meant by fidelity to a higher purpose—that purpose of loving one another.

Our Heavenly Father wants us to grow and be able to return to Him because He loves us. He knows that sometimes this mortal life, between the two gardens, is indeed treacherous and filled with deception. He knows all of us will struggle at some time in our lives. With our limited understanding, we interact with one another with merely the human heart and mind as the only tools we have to use. However, Christ will speak to our minds and souls the actions we should take to keep our minds safe and show us the way to love one another—if we let Him. Through our intentional efforts, we gain true happiness and change our very natures on our journey between two gardens…and, eventually, we enter into His love, forever.

CHAPTER 10

SCARS OF BETHESDA

Despite all of life's trials and tribulations, we can overcome most of the distraction and struggles of the natural world we live in. Life can still be pretty great; perhaps this is in part due to facing and overcoming challenges. For me, personally, the stroke has become a bittersweet moment in my life. And over time, it has grown sweeter as I continually realize I've learned lessons from the stroke that I could not have learned any other way. Our struggles take on new meaning when our struggles meet purpose.

One serendipitous outcome from my stroke is the course I quite naturally took resulting in my current position as director of the University of Utah's Stroke Rehabilitation program. In this role, I have had the unique opportunity to develop relationships with patients going through the same trials I did—some of the hardest trials of their lives. I feel I can connect with these patients in a way other physicians may not be able to because I have personal experience with the pain, fear, and anger they may be dealing with. I have found great purpose and personal growth in helping each patient go through the steps of stroke recovery. When they realize I've been through the same hard times, they gain hope that they, too, can overcome and live a full, joy-filled life. Although I am just a very imperfect human, I can also see and appreciate more fully how the Savior can succor us because He has been through *all* we are going through.

However, some people may look at my life and see a pattern of hardships, to the point where hardships become my life story. This is not so. Disappointments and tragedies occur in all our lives. This is a sad and sobering fact of life. But those disappointments don't have to remain bitter moments. They can become treasured experiences—experiences we see as sweet and that help us learn.

I would like to explore the factors in all of our lives that can transform bitter things into sweet things. In life, given a half-full glass, we can always look at the half-full side of the glass and be grateful for what we have, rather than fixate on the half-empty side. In my situation, I could dwell on the negative. I could focus on the fact that I can't run well, so I can't compete in races with my wife and girls, or even just run for exercise effectively, nor keep up with my ever-faster wife and girls. I can, however, bike, ski, and hike. These things that I can do, individually or with others, give me hope. Although I cannot do everything I once could, I can still walk effectively and do a few of those outdoor activities I love so much. The continued ability to enjoy the outdoors through hiking, biking, and skiing is truly one of my greatest blessings. Recognizing the things we can do, and being grateful for what we have, is what happy people do. They adapt to challenges and find happiness in the changes.

We can also look at the half-empty portion, ask what can be done about it, and then go to work to change the situation. The power is within us to have that attitude and make that choice, based on our own self-esteem and sense of self-worth. God has given us the agency to make that choice in how we see ourselves and our life situations. He wants all of His children to have healthy self-esteem and then work to change their individual situations for the better.

In my life, I have experienced both successes and failures. Notable examples of a permanent limitation included, among other things, my right hand's profound lack of dexterity, making impossible the practice of delicate eye surgery, as was once my goal. I have since moved on, channeling that regret into finding fulfillment in my current activities as a doctor, husband, and father.

It is easy to believe the world owes us sweetness and happiness, but that is not the way God intended things to be in our natural world, where we live by the sweat of our brows and grow by hard experiences. In fact, many of life's experiences are like walking through an overgrown rose garden: When we are in the thick of the garden, all we feel are thorn scratches and pokes, but looking out at the garden, all we can see is beauty.

Happiness in the world between the two gardens is a state of mind, heavily influenced by our expectations: what we think about what the world gives us and what we think about how life should behave. If nothing can be done about difficult situations, which is often the case, it becomes crucial to find a way to accept the situation and control our response through believing in ourselves, choosing to channel our regrets, and finding fulfillment in other activities. These other activities may end up being more fulfilling than the original course we were on, in part because of that sense of fulfillment that comes from realizing we can overcome a challenge. Also, through the Atonement of Jesus Christ, we can make peace with life's difficult situations, even when life does not work out according to our preconceived ideas. In very simple terms, we are happy if life meets our expectations. Period. The challenge we all face is adjusting, or adapting, our expectations of life and submitting to God's will with faith that He will support us. He will give us more than is sufficient for our needs.

The other day, a woman visited my office. I had not seen her for a couple of years, and she had driven a great distance to see me. Her husband had been a stroke patient of mine on the Rehabilitation Unit. Four years ago, he'd had the serious and life-threatening complication of pneumonia, about three weeks after his stroke. At the time, he had to be moved from the Rehabilitation Unit to the ICU for support for his breathing. I had already seen some early progress in his recovery. Going from the Rehab Unit to the ICU with pneumonia can be a devastating setback.

This good wife faced difficult decisions at that time—decisions that included the option to choose comfort care and "letting nature take its course." Although this is sometimes the most compassionate course, I thought it important to let this good wife know about the potential her husband had for recovery and a high quality life with her. After my visit, she decided against comfort care and opted instead for the course of rehabilitation that would eventually lead to recovery of function—of being able to live outside the hospital setting, walk with assistance, and, with help, take care of himself. I hoped this couple would have a few more good years together...which turned out to be the case.

That day of her visit was the four-year anniversary of when I came to visit them in the ICU. She told me of the many adaptations that had been necessary. He taught her it was better to be content with your situation than to be patient, waiting for something that might never come. She had come to thank me for their four wonderful years together, with her assuming the caregiver role, while his role in the family also shifted. She came to tell me he had recently died, "a wonderful death," in her arms, and that she was excited that eventually she would be reunited with him after this life was over. This remarkable woman channeled her regrets about her husband's stroke into other fulfilling activities with her husband, while maintaining a very realistic set of expectations, including expectations about life and death. Things were not the same for either spouse after his setback, but they chose to see the glass as half-full. She is a wonderful example to me—and to all of us.

Knowing the choice we all made to come to earth and be subject to "non-garden of Eden" conditions, in the natural, sometimes harsh world can help people in countless ways. The knowledge that God doesn't cause hardships, but supports us in our trials, makes an enormous difference. The knowledge that one of our life's purposes is to experience hardship and struggle, and hopefully rise, ascend, and overcome them also provides hope for me. In this way, we can figuratively and literally connect to and share in Christ's redemption. We can be enabled and strengthened through Christ's Atonement. We can figuratively *rise* with Christ in our shared ascent. We can do this right here and now. This may be the only way we can spiritually progress and come to a state of peace, contentment, and happiness.

God, in His infinite wisdom, sent us to earth to struggle, bear sickness and afflictions, experience opposites, and gain experience and joy. He sent His Only Begotten Son to gain victory and overcome this world. These points can forge an unbreakable testimony that can make a profound difference in your outlook on life. Our human subconscious mind operates essentially (though not completely) in a binary fashion—yes or no, light or dark, glass half-full or half-empty—in other words, in paired opposition. In actuality, our glass is always full, even overflowing, if we have the faith and foresight to see it, for we all will receive salvation. Having this foresight and enduring in the end in faith becomes our greatest human challenge.

In the last couple of decades, research has delved in to discover, on a neurological basis, what makes people resilient and brings them happiness. The situation becomes more complex when neurological injury is present, given the adaptions necessary as people face a long road of recovery from significant and traumatic life events such as stroke and brain injury. However, it may be that our brains are "hard-wired" for resiliency and to respond and yearn for the things that bring happiness and joy. There is now a wide and growing recognition that people may report positive as well as negative psychological changes following a traumatic event. The term "post-traumatic growth" has been applied to these perceived positive changes, sometimes called an adaptive spiral.[1]

Interestingly, the key features of resiliency and happiness are not really that complex. There are five of them:

1. Counting your blessings and recognizing the good in your life

2. Having a healthy and secure role in your family and community
3. Being socially connected
4. Engaging in physical activity and exercise
5. Finding opportunities to learn, grow, and serve others

Let's briefly explore each one of these resiliencies.

Counting your blessings. Doing so, even just once a week, forces recognition that the glass is half-full and significantly increases one's level of happiness.[2] In meditation and prayer, many faith traditions all over the world encourage this daily practice of expressing gratitude for our blessings. These daily acts serve us by allowing us to see the good in our lives and gain a greater sense of peace.

Having a healthy and secure role in your family and community. Usually, adaptations must be made after a stroke or brain injury because a major shuffling of roles and responsibilities may be necessary. However, some of the sweetest stories of love and devotion, and also struggle and hardship, result when these roles are shifting. The opportunity to slow down, maybe do some volunteer work, or travel as a couple becomes a good goal, which most, but certainly not all, stroke patients are able to reach. Again, adaptations will be necessary, but it is possible that relationships are sometimes improved after serious neurological injury.[3] Ultimately, it's up to each of us to find a role we can feel good about, one that contributes to our families and our communities. Studies show that coping with loss optimally does not only involve just "getting over it and moving on," but should also include creating meaning to facilitate the best recovery.[4] We create meaning in strong support systems and families by "providing a way to craft narratives about the changes that have occurred, and by offering perspectives that can be integrated into schema change."[5]

Being socially connected.[6] In ancient and modern times, being a member of a group or "tribe" fosters these social connections. Dr. Robert Waldinder is the present lead researcher of a project conducted over a seventy-five-year period at Harvard to learn insights into what makes humans happy. According to Waldinder, the study's main conclusion was that in the long-run, "good relationships keep us happier and healthier."[7] Apparently, our brains are wired to yearn to "love our neighbor." In a sense, deep, long-lasting friendships that aid in socialization are important to our spirits and our bodies. However, physical mobility problems often hamper the ability to socialize; thus, a good rehabilitation team will problem-solve to overcome this barrier by, for example, creating support groups and recreational groups of individuals with similar interests. Whether we are physically impaired or fully mobile, adaptations are always necessary in all our lives.

Engaging in physical activity and exercise.[8] We can literally transform our brain through intentional effort, and one of the best ways to do so is physical activity, specifically aerobic exercise. It is especially helpful when we engage in novel and varied physical activities. This effect increases, perhaps surprisingly, when the activities are done outdoors. As Walt Whitman said, "But are not exercise and the open air within the reach of us all?"[9] Even though I have to focus on the placement of each step, hiking is something that fills my soul. I know this feeling is a result of the complex neurotransmitter cascade going on in my brain, but I recognize it, too, as a gift from our Creator. The fact that our world is so beautiful and that our human brains respond and are receptive to this beauty is really a rich blessing. Input from all our senses—visual, auditory, smell, skin sensation, and taste—sends a flood of pleasure that can create a virtual symphony in our minds. It's truly remarkable.

Finding opportunities to learn, grow, and serve others.[10] These things strengthen our confidence and support our connections with the people in our communities, especially if we use our energy to look outside of ourselves and serve others.

A quote, often misattributed to Henry David Thoreau, offers this insight, "Happiness is like a butterfly; the more you chase it, the more it will elude you, but if you turn your attention to other things, it will come and sit softly on your shoulder."[11] Mother Teresa further implores, "Let no one ever come to you without leaving better and happier. Be the living expression of God's kindness: kindness in your face, kindness in your eyes, kindness in your smile."[12]

It is a challenge to behave in accordance with these five factors, but when we do, we are really taking steps toward more resiliency; we can nourish our brain to obtain additional happiness in our lives. Our lives are full of challenges, both large and small. It has been said that life, if you are on the right track, is going to be uphill. It may not be an unbearably steep uphill climb, but pushing ourselves to improve, adapt, grow, and serve others, even in the face of severe challenges, is one of the critical components to attaining happiness and a high quality of life.

As for me, facing challenges has become a large part of my life. Every day I am reminded that simple things are not as easy as they were before the stroke. However, knowing the glass is still half-full, and being able to make the necessary adaptations, I have found a great life, for which I am thankful. In my youth, I used to think faith could spare me from difficulties…but through difficult life lessons, I now know that because of difficult things, we can grow and grow closer to God. We will be able to choose to make it bitter or sweet, but that is a decision we all have to make again and again throughout our lives.

The strength to move on in spite of challenges comes partially from your own effort, which stems from what you believe in your heart and in your mind. A person's level of confidence plays a role in his or her ability to consistently grow, or from lack of confidence, give up.[13] Our own efforts, however, can and should be coupled with Christ's strength and support. Through my challenges, I have learned to lean on Christ for strength—I know, with His help, I can do things I could not do on my own. In the Book of Mormon, we read, "Nevertheless, the Lord God showeth us our weakness that we may know that it is by his grace, and his great condescension unto the children of men, that we have power to do these things" (Jacob 4:6-7). Never have I felt such weakness as at the time of my stroke. Complete and utter defeat. My life was over. I was as if dead. I fully comprehended it. I fully accepted it. Then, I made a choice, because I still had the power to choose. I started a new life. I rose. I found Christ's grace; I was enabled. I felt empowered at times to do things beyond my normal strength.

Every victory, large or small, became His. Every experience, frustrating or joyful, became His. Every experience with patients I have seen—His. All the struggles and the successes—His. Every day I live—His. Christ in me works. He invites us all to share in His grace. "For as in Adam all die, even so in Christ shall all be made alive" (1 Corinthians 15:22). Perhaps I had to give my life away in order to find it.[14] This life has blossomed into something sweet.

Consider a story from Mark's Gospel (Mark 2:1-5) of Jesus's ability to give healing through spiritual redemption, and then for physical recovery. As Jesus's popularity increased, He was sought after as a teacher and healer. On one occasion, He was teaching in a house, with multitudes of people eager to hear this new "prophet." A sick man with palsy was carried by four companions on a stretcher, probably a long distance, in hopes to be healed by Jesus. However, the crowd was too dense around the house Jesus was teaching in to navigate a stretcher. So the man's caregivers went to the extraordinary measures of removing part of the roof, and with ropes and manpower, lowering the stretcher down to Jesus. Then came the anticipated moment when all things could be set right. After all this effort by numerous people who expected a grand physical healing, Jesus said, simply, "Thy sins be forgiven thee." A spiritual redemption. What ensued were questions by the shocked critics and naysayers: "Who is this man from Galilee to think he can grant forgiveness of sins?" Blasphemous. And consider the bewilderment of the man who so desperately yearned for a cure for his palsy. I imagine this scene played out for several moments. And then came the blessing the man hoped for; Jesus said, "Take up thy bed and walk." And the man did walk, walking out of the building and walking home. What we don't know is the man's mindset before and after, as well as his physical condition: Did he walk with any type of limp? Was he bewildered or thankful and satisfied? Certainly, unplanned adaptations were required in his life to move forward. And, above all, which of the two statements by Christ would come to mean the most to him—the spiritual or the physical redemption?

We read of another of Christ's miraculous healings in John 5. Many people in Jerusalem drew their water from the Pool of Bethesda, a place I have visited because I feel reverence for what took place there two thousand years ago. This pool was rumored to have supernatural powers of healing because "an angel went down," and if one was lucky enough to be in the water when the water was "troubled" by some mystical force, the person in the water would be healed and become whole. Upon visiting this pool, Jesus saw a man; he was crippled, and alone. Jesus asked the man why he wasn't in the water, awaiting the mystical "troubling" of the waters. The man told him he didn't have anyone to carry him down to the water. To that, Jesus replied, "Take up thy bed and walk," and the man did just that (John 5:2-9). The man miraculously was physically healed, but no measure of reassurance or comfort was spoken at that time. Again, we don't know his mindset before and after: Did he walk perfectly, and was the man satisfied and whole, or would he yearn for more? What was his life like the next day, or the next month? Would it be preposterous to wonder if this physically healed man was eventually back at the same pool, wanting more? I wonder to what extent *I* have wanted more after being miraculously healed myself. Perhaps unplanned adaptations are likely necessary for all of us who have ever waited by the Pool of Bethesda to be healed physically, spiritually, or emotionally.

In the two episodes, the outcomes of the physical healing were the same, to the point of both men being able to walk by their own power and be made "whole." One can imagine only gratitude in these two men, but they were certainly not blessed with a carefree life—this is not God's pattern for dealing with His children. Perhaps in both incidents, Mark and John are trying to teach important points, and it's a lesson I learned personally.

In my case, I was reminded of a valuable concept when I received the blessing from LDS President Monson. I was thankful to receive such a special blessing when I was in need of healing. President Monson blessed me with two specific things: I would return to the medical field to bless the lives of others, and I would be able to support my family through my work. He didn't say it was going to be easy, nor that I would be completely physically whole. However, he spoke to my mind and addressed my body in exactly the way I needed to be "whole." In other words, which apply to all of us, when we go to the Lord for healing, for inspiration, for whatever we think we need, we have to trust that the Lord, Creator of bodies and minds, in His wisdom and mercy, will give us exactly what we need, even though it might not be exactly what we want or think we need. As Fiona Givens explains, "What we think we need to be happy and whole is not always what the Healer knows we need to be happy and whole." We need to trust "the Great Physician [to know] where His healing is most needed,"[15] and sometimes hand over the controls and let Him steer where He knows we need to go. We cannot petition for the great healing power and then dictate what that healing looks like. It is imperative to embrace the unplanned adaptations, and, whenever possible, avoid going back to wait by the Pool of Bethesda because our healing was not satisfactory to us.

Consider the difference between *healing* and *cure.* Cure infers a return to our previous state of wellbeing, which is usually what we long for. But the scriptures speak of the gift of healing, and never of the gift of cure. Healing is a different process from cure. As LDS author Wendy Ulrich states:

> Healing involves a spiritual and emotional reweaving of our life story to incorporate, not merely remove, our injuries. It involves growth and personal change, maturation into a new state of deep-

> er trust in God despite, but not in the absence of, suffering. It includes acceptance of our lost innocence, while reaching for greater wisdom. Healing does not mean going back to Eden, but going forward through the wounding world of mortality to a wholeness that transcends rather than excludes evil.[16]

In my own experience treating patients, I am often surprised by their resiliency of spirit and their will to live and progress. For example, CJ was a construction worker at twenty-two years of age when he fell off a landing of twenty feet. Amazingly, he popped right up and said, "Get back to work; I'm fine," but he collapsed to the ground a few moments later. Both sides of the arteries that fed his brainstem were burst, and he suffered a catastrophic stroke. Ambulances came and intubated him to begin mechanical ventilation. He quickly went from the ER to the ICU. When the doctors assessed him, they saw no signs of brain activity based on the absence of spontaneous movement. But CJ remembers the doctors telling his mother, "We ought to just turn the machines off; his brain is already dead." Luckily, his mother insisted on checking to make sure. Sure enough, his mind was still functioning adequately. Through the weeks and months that ensued, CJ did have some spontaneous recovery. He was eventually able to wean off mechanical ventilation, the machine required to breathe for him. His swallow returned so he could eat some foods, and he weaned off the feeding tube that fed his stomach. He began to have some movement of his mouth, enough to voice one-word requests. He was also able to control a computer mouse with an "eye-gaze" system, enough to write complex thoughts and expressions. He used his intact intelligence to enroll in college and complete courses.

In my clinic today, looking into CJ's intelligent eyes, broken body aside, I feel as though I'm peering into his soul, a profile of courage. One day I asked him one probing question: "Out of all the painful and trying experiences of the last nineteen years, are you still glad to be alive?" He replied, in his labored and breathy voice, with an enthusiastic "Definitely!" I perceived that if he were physically able, he would have shouted for joy in that moment. I have to wonder if, over the nineteen years, he has made the adaptations required to do the critical things for happiness, to count his blessings, thrive in a redefined social and familial role setting, learn novel ways to socialize, and gain from the sensory experience of the outdoors. If someone like CJ, in spite of losing so much, can count each day as a blessing, perhaps those of us who are not so severely afflicted can take courage by CJ's example. Perhaps the Healer knew what CJ needed to feel whole; as outside observers, we can provide support, as well as trust the Lord who knows where healing is needed most.

As a physician myself, I am conscientious of my obligation not just to prescribe a pill, but whenever possible, to help to heal a life. Healing comes from a sacred place within the mind. As the late neurosurgeon Dr. Paul Kalanithi, who died with his music still in him, but able to write an inspiring memoir, said, "The call to protect life—and not merely life but another's identity; it is perhaps not too much to say another's soul—[is] obvious in its sacredness.... Those burdens are what make medicine holy and wholly impossible: in taking up another's cross, one must sometimes get crushed by the weight."[17]

Personally, my challenge and my obligation is to bear my cross, including my neurological scars on the right side of my body, the scars of its movement, of its speech, for I know that through me, through the scars, others gain hope and confidence, and I take part in witnessing the miracle of the Lord healing their minds. I make an indelible impression, for better or worse—some people see scars of vulnerability, others see scars of strength, while, perhaps others see nothing at all. For people like the wife in the ICU contemplating giving up, the neurological scars I bear prompted hope and led to four more years with her husband. I have had to trust in the Healer of the world, Jesus Christ. He will continue to give me just the right healing for my needs and for the needs of His other children. Sometimes physicians, as well, need to trust the Great Physician—trust where His healing is needed most, and where our lives need to be steered; trust that sometimes we are to be tools in His hands, scars and all.

On the wall in my office is a large painting gifted by a grateful patient. Its subject matter meant a lot to this patient, and over the five years since the gift was given, it has grown to mean more perhaps to me than to her. It is of a young woman performing a beautiful dance, while other dancers look on. My patient was a dancer in her youth, and she enjoyed dancing recreationally until her late forties when a stroke partially paralyzed one side of her body and left her with lack of coordination. She struggled to walk, let alone dance. After working with her on the Rehabilitation Inpatient Unit, and for months in the outpatient clinic, she eventually met milestones like returning to driving, and then returning to working at the bank part-time, then full-time in the manager's position she had previously held. She made successful adaptations for these things, probably hundreds of adaptations to her life. Each time I saw her, I thought, "What a remarkable recovery. She is really making the most of her life." However, what I did not know about was the dancing. She presented me with a poem that she wrote, along with the gift. The poem reads:

> Strangers, brought together at desperate times.
>
> You took me in at my worst.
>
> With watchful, non-judgmental eyes, and tender loving hands.
>
> You held me up and cared for me, until I could dance once more.
>
> You steady me for the outside world with quiet, guiding thoughts.
>
> You readied my heroes so that they might continue the dance with me.
>
> All this could never really be repaid,
>
> Knowing this, you continue your valiant effort.
>
> Saying thank you doesn't seem to bring it justice.

> Therefore, in remembrance of this, each day, I work to redefine my dance.
>
> I hope that someday, perhaps, even a portion of everything you have done for us can be returned to you.

Her dance was not as it once was, but her dance through life has been more meaningful, now that she has had to struggle for everything she has regained. I, acting as her unwitting guide through this chapter of her life, played a more powerful role because of my experience with stroke, and the scars, which I try to carry well with me.

Over the last many years, I have been making great efforts to hide these scars. We all carry these scars of some sort or another; maybe showing them can strengthen those around us. Because hiding them is a little like hiding a light under a bushel. Have I not outlined the neurological formula for happiness—the five resiliencies listed above that demonstrate God's ability to heal our minds? Don't I benefit personally from those five discoveries? I have made adaptations to count my blessings and see the glass is half-full, I have created a meaningful niche in my social and family roles, I have had opportunities to socialize, and I gain from the sensory experience of being active in the outdoors. Shouldn't I be shouting for joy, as CJ has so aptly taught me? Or will I hide my light that emanates from the scars of Bethesda under a bushel? For me, the answer is "No." I trust in Jesus Christ, Healer of the world, to give me and His children the succor we need, and I will gladly carry the scars of Bethesda for His purposes—on the path, between two gardens.

CHAPTER 11

RELATIONSHIPS, GOOD INTENTIONS, AND CONSEQUENCES IN OUR NATURAL WORLD

Despite my impairments, I maintain a fairly active lifestyle. It's important to me to be a part of the healthy and active population, especially outdoors. In nature, I believe we can see the handiwork of the perfect artist. Indeed, as LDS President Gordon B. Hinckley explained, "All of beauty in the earth bears the fingerprints of the Master Creator."[1]

As I tried out various forms of activities, given my physical limitations after my stroke, I knew returning to cycling was a risk since my right side is partially paralyzed and I'm on blood thinners. However, I picked my routes, avoided traffic, and tried to be as cautious as possible. I liked riding in the canyon, Emigration Canyon up to "Big Mountain," specifically. I enjoyed being at the high summit, perched as if at the top of the world, looking down on the vast wilderness mountains so close to Salt Lake City. The descent from Big Mountain, with its steep, smooth, and fast terrain, feels much like, not biking, but soaring on a smooth carbon frame and two sleek, narrow tires, like a bird—but, in this case, with other forms of wildlife, including big game. Perhaps, like Icarus of old, I was flying too close to the sun, with wings of wax, or, in my case, with a single wing of wax.

On a beautiful evening at twilight in June of 2016, the freak accident occurred. I was soaring down Emigration Canyon from Big Mountain at a high rate of speed—over 40 miles per hour. Out of the corner of my eye, I saw a deer coming out of the bushes into the road. I don't remember much of anything at all for the next couple of hours, but a friend saw the following events transpire. The deer struck me on my ribs and torso with such force that it broke most of my ribs on my left side. The impact knocked me off the road and sent me careening down the steep embankment. I eventually crashed, unconscious, in the underbrush and reeds around the creek. Were it not for my friend, Rob, with whom I had been riding that day, I probably would have lain there until morning and conceivably not survived. Rob is probably responsible for saving my life because he summoned help. The paramedics arrived, closed the road, and took me to the ER at the University Hospital. If Rob wasn't riding with me, and specifically riding behind me, I could have spent the night in the cold canyon in the ravine and died of exposure. I realize there were tender mercies that night.

By the time I started forming "new" memories, after the characteristic retrograde amnesia from the concussion subsided, I was well into my emergency room visit, having no actual memory of the accident, extraction, ambulance ride, or half of the ER stay. Thus began a three-week stay in the hospital, including ten days in the ICU. I was truly fortunate to miss only six weeks of work, but my treatment, therapy, and recovery went on for months. Eventually, my spirit was revived and I was healed, or at least back to my baseline functional capacity.

With this new trauma, I again went through the stages of recovery, with some new and some old issues resurfacing. I essentially had to relearn how to walk once again, relying on the medical knowledge and faith that my strength and my sensation on the right side would return. What's more, I had put my family and our goals at risk because this accident could have easily led to permanent disability or death. As a family, we went through justifiable and understandable resentment as we each had to make sense of what had happened in our own way.

Unexpectedly, for many months, I struggled with a form of muscle tightness, called spasticity, which, for a time, made my muscles uncoordinated and hard to control. On the positive side, I gained new insight and an appreciation for the subtle but sometimes significant issues that surround muscle spasticity, which affects a large portion of my stroke population—a good thing for a stroke rehabilitation doctor to understand and appreciate.

Going through this experience, I again had time for introspection—to contemplate life, our purpose here, and especially that we are on earth "two by two," as couples and in family units. We don't live in isolation. I don't know if it was necessary for me to learn that lesson by putting my family through trauma again, but it's a lesson, nonetheless, that has been reinforced. Traumatic events happen because we are having mortal experiences. We live in the natural world God created, being subject to His natural laws. I don't believe for a second that God caused that collision with the deer. Nevertheless, that terrible accident affected not only myself, but also those I love the most.

Knowing that what we do often impacts those who love us more than it affects us presents some challenges. It's true that Emi and I have had to strengthen, toughen, and stabilize ourselves as individuals. We have tried to make sense of our lives in the context of being a couple and going through these distressing events.

That we are here in families allows for rich experiences to love and care about others deeply. Interactions with loved ones can be deeply rewarding, and also challenging at times. As a couple, Emi and I have had unforeseen pain and struggles, and rain-soaked days (maybe more than our share). We have also experienced love and joy; this, too, maybe more than our share.

When you are in a committed relationship like marriage, experiences that happen to one member invariably affect the other member, sometimes in ways imperceptible to the other person. When I had my stroke, it started a lifetime of adjustments and accommodations for both myself and Emi. With time, I learned to adjust to the stroke's impairments until these adjustments became second nature to me. I may even admit to feeling a sense of pride at having overcome so much. But for my spouse, my impairments have taken a different toll throughout our marriage.

About two years after my stroke, Emi and I decided to do a rather ambitious hike in the Tetons near Jackson, Wyoming. We planned the route from the top of the aerial tram at Teton Village and then planned to hike down Granite Canyon, a hike of about 4,200 vertical feet over thirteen miles. The first half of the hike was beautiful, enjoyable, and awesome. About halfway down, however, my right big toe began to hurt. As time went on, it became more and more painful, as my toenail butted up against the toe of my very hard boot. I had to walk more and more slowly because of the now excruciating pain with every step in my stroke-impaired right toe. After a few hours of this extremely slow pace, Emi commented to me, "You know, it's not easy for me to walk this slowly."

When we finally arrived at the car and took my boot off to see a bloody and swollen big toe, the toenail black and partially off, I didn't understand her seemingly obtuse comment. I was in so much physical pain and anguish that I couldn't see past my own self to see Emi's point of view. It's taken me many years to comprehend and appreciate the fact that, like this hike, this experience with my stroke was difficult for both of us. Life continues to be difficult on a daily basis for Emi because she has a husband who is not physically whole. Perhaps it is more difficult for her than for me. That realization has taken a long time to wrap my head around. However, my impression and understanding is that Emi's experience, being the spouse without the stroke, or accident, or cancer, or any number of things, is not unique; it is more common than people might think, even universal.

Spouses often feel a greater sense of being wrapped-up in emotions over what has happened and what the future may hold. They may also feel like the one in the background—the one always picking up the pieces. They may even feel a sense of loss for some of the elements that were part of their marriage before a stroke or other life-changing event. Honesty in marriage is fundamentally important; however, honesty and absolute transparency may get confused.

In matters pertaining to the unique way we each make sense of the world (no two people are exactly alike in the body of Christ), it may be both a matter of respecting privacy and an act of caring to keep some things sacred with the Lord. We can respect our spouse's honor and peace of mind. For example, Emi does not make it a point to tell me how wonderful it would be if I were physically able to go on a morning run with her, just like Sarah didn't point out that Abraham had wrinkly and withered skin in his old age. Absolute transparency and hostility can sometimes live side by side; one has to consider the preservation of the loved one's honor and peace of mind. In other words, not all transparency is uplifting in a relationship, and it is not the primary goal—Christ is. Learning to love like Christ may be a lifelong journey. Honor and respect are certainly necessary in a consecrated marriage, a marriage with Christ at its head. Emi and I both attempt to put Christ at the center of our lives together, while caring for the other's feelings.

Having Christ at the center becomes even more important when facing the loss of a loved one. No loss came at quite so high a price for us as losing our precious baby, Eliza, who was stillborn. Three years later, we suffered devastation at the hand of my stroke. We were both doing our best with this new set of mortal challenges. For Emi, it meant trying to keep our family afloat with a husband working doctor's hours and being less able to do the normal and expected "heavy lifting" around the home.

The two individuals who make up a couple have different strengths to bring to a relationship, including in times of loss. As such, couples complement and supplement each other in such a way that the sum is greater than its parts. It may be a challenge to some to realize that these differences can strengthen a couple. Perhaps as both spouses recognize the unique strengths their spouse brings to the marriage, they each gain more flexibility. Our first parents, Adam and Eve, apparently had very different personalities. Adam, I imagine, lived "by the book," checked the boxes, and sat in the front pew. Alternately, I imagine Eve saw the "big picture" and was more interested in growth and connections. However, they eventually learned to live in harmony with one another. By first acknowledging their differences, couples can learn to appreciate the various ways to look at and solve life's problems.

In our own lives, for example, Emi has yearned for me, her husband, to do the daily expressions of faith that she finds meaningful, such as daily scripture study. I, on the other hand, perhaps erroneously, have felt I was already daily engaged on the Lord's errand by providing medical care to people trying to regain their lives after horrific tragedies. However, after hearing her urgings and the recommendations from prophets and apostles, I did incorporate daily scripture study into my life. Although I am not perfect in studying daily, I now recognize the blessings that can only come as a result of frequent immersion in the scriptures, pondering it throughout the day, and receiving inspiration from it for my life. I thank Emi for providing the encouragement that enhances my life. I do believe that, often, some of these differences we have as couples, including attitudes, insights, and approaches, can be cherished and celebrated. In this way, we can all strengthen marriage because of the diversity and validity of looking at problems from various angles.

Emi and I have used faith and the example of the Savior's love as a compass to guide us. We have been able to let this love survive, grow, and flourish throughout the challenges we have faced. I count this as a great gift, even a miracle equal to how I survived the crash when deer met bike.

I face the constant challenges of deciding what measures are necessary to keep me safe. Of course, there is risk in outdoor activities as there is in life. For most of us, the most dangerous thing we do on a routine basis is drive a car. Outdoor activities are perhaps a little more risky in my case. When I get injured, it takes me longer than normal to bounce back. I don't want to have undue risk in my life, but I also don't want to live in fear. I suppose we all live with a variety of inconsistencies. It's striking, the paradox of wanting to ride the bike, but not wanting to be injured again. Of wanting to be cautious and not take chances, but not wanting to live in fear. Of wanting to love without restraint, but not wanting to be vulnerable or get hurt. Reconciling these paradoxes becomes one of life's delicate challenges. Taking into account the people I love and cherish, and protecting them from the pain or trauma I may cause, is a balancing act—an act I take very seriously. As a couple and as a family, we must reconcile what is acceptable and unacceptable risk, while allowing everyone to live to their full potential.

This verse from a poem penned by James Montgomery in 1826 resonates with me deeply. The poem was set to music and the name changed to "A Poor Wayfaring Man of Grief."[2] At times in our lives, both Emi and myself, have felt like both people in this passage. From the lines in the verse:

> Stript, wounded, beaten nigh to death,
>
> I found him by the highway side,
>
> I roused his pulse, brought back his breath,
>
> Revived his spirit, and supplied
>
> Wine, oil, refreshment—he was healed.
>
> I had myself a wound concealed,
>
> But from that hour forgot the smart,
>
> And peace bound up my broken heart.

Perhaps most of us have had to play the part of both people in this verse at one time or another. To me, it reinforces that we are all full of passions, bound by caution, and connected in this human family as couples, brothers, and sisters. What happens to one happens to all. We all must deal with the laws of nature that are sometimes dangerous to our fragile human bodies. Our human emotional response is one of the challenges we all continually live with and grow from on our journey, between two gardens.

CHAPTER 12

HEARTS KNIT TOGETHER IN UNITY WITH OUR NEIGHBOR

We are told to keep our "eye single to the glory of God" (D&C 4:5). But what is God's glory, His work and glory? Moses 1:39 clearly states, "this is my work and my glory—to bring to pass the immortality and eternal life of man." Ultimately, we and our exaltation are His work and glory. The Savior taught this penultimate principle when he expounded on the "Two Great Commandments"—first, to love the Lord, and second, to love thy neighbor. When Christ described these two commandments, one man challenged him, saying, "And who is my neighbor?" Jesus then gave the beloved parable of the Good Samaritan. "Which now of these three, thinkest thou, was the neighbor unto him that fell among the thieves?... He that shewed mercy on him.... Go and do likewise" (Luke 10:36-37). When we care and serve our fellow men and women, our "neighbors," we are keeping our eye single to His glory. We are caring for others in concrete and tangible ways, acting in His stead to show a measure of God's love. In this way, our hearts can be knit together in unity.

Emi, a couple of friends, and I had an experience in 1998 (which now seems like a lifetime ago) that taught us a little about the term "neighbors." Emi and I were living on the outskirts of Chicago where I was attending medical school and Emi was working. The University of Utah was coming to town to play a basketball game against Wake Forrest, led by Tim Duncan at the United Center, and we were excited to go see the game. People from Chicago know that the United Center is surrounded by some well-known projects, built in the late '50s, called the Henry Horner Homes. These neighborhoods are a haven for crime and drugs. There is a parking lot on the United Center campus, with strong, fifteen-foot fences surrounding the lot, but the cost to safely park your car there for the evening is twenty-five dollars. However, literally right across the street is an unfenced, open parking lot that charges only eight dollars. Being students, the choice was clear—we went for the less-expensive option.

While we looked for a parking space in the unprotected lot, a young man in a hoody walked past my open window, and at the last moment, reached inside and punched me in the head, then ran off. It was a grazing blow that confused me more than anything else. I wondered why on earth he had done this, and we decided to go park elsewhere. However, before we could exit the lot, the young man reappeared. I remembered a similar experience Apostle Dallin H. Oaks shared years ago, about a night when he was in Chicago, and a would-be robber in a similar part of town demanded money and his car keys at gunpoint. He received the prompting that only bad things would happen to him and the young boy if he tried to overtake the robber.[1] Similarly, a clear prompting came to me, "Don't get out of the car." I felt only bad things would happen to me, Emi, the two friends with us in the backseat, and the young boy if I confronted him outside the car. As the young man rushed toward our car, I locked the door and rolled up the window just in time. I could see the whites of his very aggressive eyes. Before I could maneuver my car and escape, he tried to kick in the window three times, but we were able to drive away physically unscathed. As we drove away, we noticed a van parked nearby with a number of young men who looked like they were ready to pounce on us. We escaped, but we were emotionally shaken.

I was quite troubled by the experience, and I had a hard time making sense of it. I was now feeling animosity toward a whole segment of the population with different skin color than my own—animosity that was not in my nature. I needed to understand why my life had intersected with this young man's in such a violent and negative way. In the days that followed, a friend gave me a book detailing the experiences of those living in the Horner Homes. *There Are No Children Here* talks of the Third-World conditions, gang violence, drug abuse, rampant teenage pregnancies, and fatherless families that have spanned generations in these homes.[2] With conflicts between gangs like the Gangster Disciples and the Black Rangers, the homicide rate in the neighborhood was ten times that of the rest of Chicago.[3] That young man's violent, brief interaction with me could have been part of his gang initiation.

Nonetheless, I wanted to go back; I felt I had to go back; I needed to avoid allowing this one bad experience to make a lasting impression. It's as if, in order to stay all right by God, I would first have to get right with this young man. The contrast between my white privilege and the plight of some of God's other children quite literally hit me square in the jaw. Could it be that God allows these types of interactions so we can choose whether to be bitter or empathetic? I found a homeless shelter in the area and arranged to go there with the youth of our ward to render service at the soup kitchen. It was becoming clear that if I wanted to feel reconciled to God—to be exalted and become like Christ—I would need to keep my eye on His children's welfare.

Terryl and Fiona Givens speak about our absolute reliance on creating and developing meaningful relationships with other people as a requirement to progress and receiving exaltation. They say, "We create meaningful bonds and connections by what we specifically do with and for others."[4] I realized this means all of His children, including those who don't look like me, or are from other backgrounds, including other races.

Terryl Givens points out that Joseph Smith had a vision of heaven in which "honorable men and women of the earth are saved in a kingdom of glory but are not in the Father's presence. Not because they do not 'deserve' it or qualify for it but because, given the opportunity, they have not yet created that relationship with God."[5] It seems reasonable to say that one way—maybe the main way—we create a relationship with God is by loving and serving our neighbor.

Developing the ability to create meaningful relationships with "God and man" is one of the main reasons we're here on earth. We get closer to God when we embrace his children's needs. After all, "insomuch as ye have done unto the least of these, ye have done it unto me" (Matthew 25:40).

Although that young boy and I will likely never meet on the earth again, our paths diverged after that brief encounter. I knew that young boy was at high risk of eventually being imprisoned or dying young from other gang-related activities. However, I am very thankful for the Gospel plan that will enable me one day, in heaven, to greet that young man from Chicago as my brother, eye to eye, with clear understanding. I am also thankful for a gospel plan that ties us all together and requires us to love one another in order to progress and draw closer to our Father in Heaven. And I'm thankful for the experiences we have individually and within our families, ward families, and communities—experiences that bring us great joy, but we also have to struggle through, both individually and collectively—struggles that enrich our lives.

While in medical school before my stroke, my LDS congregation public relations advisor asked me to accompany him on a speaking engagement at the small Wheaton College, a Christian college and home to the Billy Graham organization's headquarters. We were to speak to a class that compared different religions and the different Christian denominations. I had been home just three years from my LDS mission to Japan, so I was comfortable speaking to groups about the almost universal experiences of faith journeys. The assigned topic was "The Mormons' View of Christ," a topic I have a deep and strong feeling about. We were aware that this class had a certain set of predispositions against the "Mormon Christ." Furthermore, the last person to present to this group had talked about the Jehovah's Witness view of Christ, and in subsequent lectures, that view was scoured and excoriated. In spite of the various methods by which faith cultures approach religion, I reminded them that most people worship the same God, even if going about it in different ways. I spoke first, and began by posing the question to the class, "What are your beliefs on who Christ is?"—in the spirit of building on common beliefs. We had a wonderful discussion. It was clear to all present that neither they nor I had all the answers concerning God's mysteries, but we all had enormous points of agreement. Bridges were built where there once were walls. Both sides were firm in their testimony of Christ. I felt God's peace and His presence.

Following the lecture, we attended a previously arranged lunch and a chance to discuss the topic further with a few student leaders. I felt at home on that campus and among those students, just as I had during my undergraduate work at Brigham Young University (BYU). The students were well groomed and articulate. They told me they had signed an honor code, similar to the one at BYU. We had an enjoyable talk about the common elements in our religious views and cultures. At the end of our time together, I asked a pointed question. I had heard throughout the years that evangelist Christians could not accept the LDS view of Christ and the belief that His doctrine is sufficient to allow salvation; thus, evangelist Christians believe members of the Church of Jesus Christ of Latter-day Saints are destined to damnation. I wanted to ask these intelligent students, with whom I had developed a friendship, the ultimate question: "Based on my testimony and belief in Christ, what will it be—salvation or damnation for me?" They replied, though I perceived it pained them to admit it, that they had to adhere to their belief that Latter-day Saints were destined for damnation.

The point of these examples may be that it makes a tremendous difference whether you view other people as doomed for eternal damnation or as future neighbors in heavenly mansions. I am discovering that love is always an option. I am discovering that love, above all else, makes the difference in our interactions. Our human challenge is to develop the capacity to love, without fear, without anxiety, and certainly without hate, in every situation and circumstance. I firmly believe Paul when he says, "For I am persuaded, that neither death, nor life, nor angels, nor principalities, nor powers, nor things present, nor things to come, nor height, nor depth, nor any other creature, shall be able to separate us from the Love of God, which is in Christ Jesus our Lord" (Romans 8:38-39). To love each other in this way is what we should all aspire to.

This bias against Mormons and the reasoning behind it was surprising to me. It challenged my views of people, even people of faith. Even though I had gained good rapport, respect, and even love for the students there, sometimes dogma gets in the way, leading to unnecessary divisiveness. It's noteworthy that these kinds of rifts play out in cultures, religions, and even families. Today, a couple of decades after my interactions with the students at Wheaton College, my understanding of the human condition—heart and mind, intermeshed with my own unique experiences—gives a little more illumination to these situations we all may find ourselves in. We get confused and distracted from the two great commandments, and as Jesus taught, all the other commandments flow from them. It couldn't be simpler: to love God, and to love your neighbor. But so often we lose sight of those commandments. Good, well-intentioned, intelligent, honest people, just trying to figure things out, often falter, given the limitations of our very human minds. But if we dwell on the details that people disagree on, like the young students at the college, we will occasionally continue to feel like a deep chasm exists between us. Bridging these various gaps with insight, understanding, and wisdom becomes a lifetime pursuit.

I developed a meaningful relationship about ten years after my stroke with a young attorney in Jackson, Wyoming, named Brian. He is also an avid biker, and had completed nine Lotoja (Logan, Utah to Jackson Hole, Wyoming) races before we met. During his tenth year participating in the 207-mile race, around the 135-mile mark, he began having visual disturbances in his right eye. He thought this odd, but he kept riding. A few moments later, he veered, lost his balance, and crashed. The emergency responders quickly assessed that a stroke had taken him down.

I first met Brian on the neurology floor at the University of Utah Medical Center soon after his stroke. He was beginning to generate speech, but he was still very weak on the right side. In subsequent days, I talked to him about the recovery process and about setting some short- and long-term goals, something I try to do with all my patients. He said he wanted to bike again. I told him that as a stroke survivor myself, biking is one of the few activities that is not only possible for a person with stroke-related weakness, but for which one can gain a high level of proficiency. He was still not walking without assistance at that time; nevertheless, I said a return to biking was a reasonable long-term goal. Twenty months later, he was planning to complete the portion of Lotoja he hadn't finished, that last seventy miles from Thayne to Jackson, Wyoming. He wanted us to do it together, patient and doctor. I eagerly made arrangements and set my own goals, including getting in better shape on my bike, gathering a team, getting jerseys, etc. True to his word, Brian got on his bike twenty months later and together we rode. Twelve people from Salt Lake and twelve people from Jackson rode that day, including my brother Mark and two of my brothers-in-law, Chad and Jon Dalton.

To say this experience meant a lot to me would be a gross understatement. Although each of us may have been on different points along the faith and belief spectrum, whatever preconceptions and prejudices could have existed were stripped away. No thoughts on either side about judging the other group as "destined for damnation" were present. That would have been inconceivable. We were all the children of the One God, under the bright blue dome, as we finished at the base of the magnificent and inspiring Teton Mountains. Light from Heaven shown down on us that day, our hearts knit together, united in purpose and love.

As humans, we all have wounds—physical, emotional, and sometimes neurological—but we have strength when we are bound together in love and purpose. Ernest Hemingway said, "The world breaks every one, and afterward, many are strong at the broken places."[6] Even being broken. . .perhaps because of being broken, we can be strong.

When Book of Mormon prophet Nephi had a vision of the Tree of Life, he learned that the fruit of that tree represents "the love of God, which sheddeth itself abroad in the hearts of the children of men; wherefore, it is the most desirable above all things" (1 Nephi 11:22), and that this love is the greatest of gifts. We also know, from the Two Great Commandments, how important love must be in God's great Plan of Happiness. Sometimes love is all that really matters in our journey between two gardens. Perhaps love is always the most important thing that matters. At times, love is the only thing we have on our journey. Though separated by the span of the great state of Wyoming, and brought together by a random coincidental health crisis, Brian and his friends became my neighbors that day, as we all lifted up each other to serve one another, to help accomplish a goal, and to strengthen ourselves and our relationships with others...with slightly different backgrounds. That day, we formed a bond that will last a lifetime. I feel as though we were able to partake of some of the fruit of the Tree of Life that sunny day, beneath the Tetons, with heaven smiling upon us.

As it turned out, we finished minutes before the "elite" racers, and the contrast between the two scenes was significant. Dozens, maybe hundreds, of people had come out from the local community to support Brian and our team. We had only done the last seventy miles, but at the finish line, everyone was elated, sharing the thrill of Brian's accomplishment. A few minutes later, the first two elite racers sped in, and a much smaller group greeted them. The man who had won, exhausted, after riding 207 miles, expressed disappointment because he had missed the record by twenty-five seconds. Two different races, two different outcomes, and remarkably different attitudes about what had just transpired. We were part of a courageous miracle.

This experience with Brian was a powerful reminder to me of why I went into medicine in the first place: for the rare opportunity to help someone—literally and figuratively—finish the race and reach a long-term goal. I am thankful to Brian; because of his courage and fortitude, we were all able to share in God's glory that day.

Studies have shown that we experience more joy when we cooperate and work together in teams than when we compete with everyone around us or isolate ourselves and choose to work alone. Personally, these experiences remind me why I fought my way back after my stroke, why I made the long journey, and why I feel compelled to assist others going through similar trials, and on to victory.

The Apostle Paul admonished, "By love serve one another" (Galatians 5:13), and King Benjamin explained, "When ye are in the service of your fellow beings ye are only in the service of your God" (Mosiah 2:17). We can look to the Savior, who helped the sick and afflicted, those destitute in both body and spirit, and who gave his life for our salvation in the perfect act of love that all spirits may be victorious. Today, the work of helping men and women rise and walk is just as miraculous, but it usually requires a little more time and effort. However, it is an absolute honor to assist in this process.

To have the chance to play an actual role in a redemption story is quite possibly among the sweetest human experiences we can have in our lifetime. Figuratively, I do realize people struggle with all manner of ailments, physically and emotionally, outside of the circumstances that bring them to my neurology floor. Certainly, we all have had times when we have needed Christ's healing power, like at the Pool of Bethesda, to heal our physical or emotional wounds. My own recovery has been an absolute miracle, but not an instant one—over years and decades, it's been a miracle I am trying to live up to every day. Now, I am witness to miracles every day, as I work to serve my neighbors and lift up the hearts that sorrow. We can all find miracles in our daily lives; this healing is open to all people, physically or spiritually, to help us all rise to meet our God-given potential with hearts knit together as one. In so doing, we can act in the stead of God to bring about His work and His glory. There may be nothing sweeter in this world. Perhaps, the greater the struggle, the sweeter the victory and joy.

CHAPTER 13

LOVE IS THE REASON FOR OUR TRAVAILS BETWEEN TWO GARDENS

Much like consciousness—that hard to explain reality that bathes our entire human experience—the concept of love is equally difficult for scientists and philosophers to explain. What are the rational reasons behind this emotion? Yet, love is. It's all around us; it bathes our human experience. In the Bible, we are taught that "God is love" (1 John 4:8). Thus, anyone who has felt the undeniable emotion of love may know that love can become a seed of faith, which, through nurturing, may grow.

Apostle Dieter F. Uchtdoft said, "Since the beginning of time, love has been the source of the highest bliss and the heaviest burdens."[1] More that the mortal mind can comprehend, "God…fills our hearts with breathtaking joy, brightens our darkest hour with blessed peace, distills on our minds precious truths, shepherds us in times of distress, rejoices when we rejoice, and answers our righteous petitions…. For what we love determines what we seek. What we seek determines what we think or do. What we think and do determines who we are—and who we will become…. But, Oh, how we need the love of God."[2]

From the time of Adam to the present, the human family has been endowed with a few noteworthy beneficial conditions. Our Heavenly Father, it seems, restored consciousness to our first parents on earth, thereby enabling in them the freedom to choose. As a human family, in the pre-mortal existence, we all chose the Savior's plan. On earth, the veil and consciousness seem to have been necessary for us to choose faith (or choose not to exercise faith), thereby enabling us to be recipients of Christ's grace, which will strengthen us to change our own circumstances for the better. When we continue to show love to God and our fellow men and women, that strength increases. Growth is achieved in this way, as we continue on a virtuous cycle that eventually leads to exaltation.

This process begins in each individual's mind, the magnificent brain God first gave to Adam, and He enlivened Adam's mind through the Breath of Life. "We are created in the image of Heavenly Parents; we are God's spirit children. Therefore, we have a vast capacity for love—it is part of our spiritual heritage," says Dieter F. Uchtdorf. And when that wonderful day of exaltation arrives, "He offers to His children the promise of a glorious and infinite existence and has provided a way for us to progress in knowledge and glory until we receive a fullness of joy. He has promised us all that He has."[3]

Our Heavenly Father has promised us so much. We should probably all feel joyful about these promises—all of the time. However, we often don't notice that this love is present in our lives, even ubiquitously present, much like animals that live their lives submerged in the sea would find it difficult to describe what water feels like—this love is the substance we are bathed in. It permeates and penetrates the deepest recesses of our lives. Yet, even though this love carries with it critical information—direction, guidance, and a roadmap of the way back to God's presence—as mortals beings, we are ill-equipped to receive the information. When we do have a powerful manifestation of God's love, we often call it a "spiritual experience." Indeed, some of us can feel the spirit powerfully on a daily basis, while others have only felt it occasionally, but can remember back to this feeling, which sustains them. Others may never have that powerful manifestation of God's love, but will have to rely more fully on faith. Whatever the case, having powerful, daily, tangible, faith-promoting experiences is not the norm; God likely does not intend for His children to have these concrete evidences of His love or even of His presence. This must be by design; otherwise, our path would be clear, rendering choice, free will, and faith obsolete, and defeating the purpose of God's plan for His children's exaltation.

However, God wants us to recognize the presence of love in our lives. Perhaps this is why Christ stressed the command to love our neighbor. The human mind needs to feel non-ethereal, but tangible, visual, and concrete love. That love happens between people, who then eventually realize that God is the author of that love. Christ no longer has any hands on this earth, except for ours. He has no eyes nor lips on this earth, except for ours. On earth, our hearts being knit together in unity is often the method God uses to show love to us. "By this shall men know, ye are my disciples, if ye have love, one to another" (John 13:35). Though imperfect humans in every way, perhaps our ability to love is the only thing we can do perfectly.

Still, we will see this love more clearly at that solemn meeting in the garden, after we put off these mortal frailties, with the fears and pains of this life forever over. Then we will see with more clarity the hero that Jesus Christ always was, is, and always will be. Until then, we are all living between two gardens.

The first time Emi and I visited Leigh Lake near Jackson, long before my stroke, we were newlyweds out for a short day-hike. I remember the majestic Teton Mountains rising above the shallow lake's crystal blue waters. Since then, Leigh Lake has become a special place for us; we went back each year of our young marriage until my stroke. On that first day at the lake, the scene was awe-inspiring to me, but for naïve and simple reasons. Swimming in the cool waters, surrounded by the majesty of the mountains and in nature, with eagles soaring overhead, and being alone with Emi was like heaven on earth. Maybe mortals can visit Eden, if only occasionally. This was before critical hardships, before entering the crucible, from another lifetime.

A few years later, our lives changed, with the stillborn birth of Eliza and then with my stroke. Immediately after the stroke, I lay helpless in my bed in the intensive care unit with nothing to do but think and remember. With the right side of my body completely paralyzed, I thought about how my life might change. What would the future hold? What would give my life meaning? Where was God in all this turmoil and suffering? In my ICU bed, feeling like life had just crashed down on me, and wondering if I was doomed to be crushed by the weight, I thought about Leigh Lake. It gave me hope. I thought of what it would take to get me back there. Would I only be capable of going there in my mind, reliving the memories of the scenic splendor I had once long ago experienced? At that time, it was hard to imagine being able to control the heavy excess baggage my entire right side had become. I thought of all-terrain wheels to attach to my hospital bed. I thought about being pushed in a cart or maybe being able to operate an electric wheelchair. Although it was hard to conceive at the time, I dared to hope I could make the hike on my own power, to feel the soothing water and the fresh warm air, and to bask in the beauty of this glorious scene. LDS President Spencer W. Kimball stated, "There are great challenges ahead…give me this mountain, give me these challenges."[4] I didn't ask for these challenges, but I knew what I had to do to attempt to meet them—to climb the mountain before me, to have the faith at least to try.

I will admit that in the aftermath of my stroke I struggled to find purpose in my and my family's challenges. Throughout my recovery experience, I knew challenging conditions were a central feature of our life on earth. I was also beginning to grasp that God allows challenges as part of the plan to provide experiences for growth. Things were just beginning to become clear—changes in perspective, changes in the practices of living in faith and of relying on the Lord to lead. Still, the pieces didn't fit seamlessly; gaping holes still existed in my picture of the world and of life. Even after three years, vague but critical unanswered questions remained. The struggle continued, both spiritually and physically. However, looking back, I was continually drawing strength and sustenance from my sense of God's love for me as one of His children. The realization and impact of this love did not come immediately, like a massive wave sweeping me off my feet. This love descended on me gradually, but it became undeniable, and has become a precious treasure.

Three years after my stroke, I was finally able to return to the magnificent scene of Leigh Lake. Returning to the place I had imagined in my mind so often made it feel like I had been there a million times before. It was a familiar, very comfortable feeling—like a homecoming. Returning to this special place held tremendous significance for me, especially in sharing this place with my precious daughters, four-year-old Ella and six-month-old Louisa. The hike to Leigh Lake, at the base of the glorious Teton Mountains, was truly spectacular; we soaked up the beauty of the natural surroundings. As I held hands with Ella, we moved along the trail, rising over gentle slopes and then down again. With Emi toting Louisa in her arms, we stopped frequently for Ella to climb up a tree stump or pick up an especially smooth stone. The four-mile round trip is perfect for small children, and I was happy to show my girls this amazing location. It was such a magnificent day—a day that held special meaning for me.

Even now, I remember wading out to waist deep, the water a refreshing contrast to the warm air. I remember going out a hundred yards until the shallow lake, with sand underfoot, rose up to the level of the water lapping against my bottom lip. Again, surrounded by the majesty of the mountains and in nature, with eagles soaring overhead, maybe Eden was still occasionally within my reach, if only to visit.

Moving farther still, I tried to get as invisible as possible. I tilted my head back; the water was covering my mouth. Only my nose and my eyes were visible—and I took it in, I inhaled it, and I consumed this awesome scene.

Looming large above me was Mount Moran, towering 6,000 feet. Its giant, rugged granite peak gave way to an enormous vertical couloir with a glacier high over my head like a massive granite wall. The slope turned less vertical about midway down the mountain, allowing evergreen trees and some bushes to take root. As the slope continued down, I saw massive boulders at the bottom of the mountain, just before the mountain seemed to slip under the lake's blue waters.

I felt small.

With my body almost entirely submerged next to the immense mass of stone, I was an insignificant speck in a vast universe. It was completely still and silent. The silence took me back again—back to the time when I felt insignificant and immaterial, yet a time when I suffered in silence. The reverence I felt for life and for nature humbled me. I tried to live in both worlds for a moment—both gardens.

Out of the sunny sky, a gentle rain began to fall. With my eyes exactly at the level of the mirror-smooth water, I could see the raindrops create small ripples as they tenderly fell from the sky. I felt completely enmeshed with nature, with life, and with living. The beauty all around me, of this earth, overwhelmed me. I felt grateful. Grateful for this beautiful world. Grateful for my half-broken body. Grateful for a second chance to have experiences like this. Grateful for a loving God.

From the shore some 100 yards away, Emi called to me. The sound was a spark, awakening me from my trance-like state. It was time to return to them, pack up our things, and go. I began the journey toward the shore.

The lake's floor was composed of fine silt that oozed between my toes with each step. Just below the surface of this soft, silt blanket were occasional rough stones with jagged surfaces and sharp edges. As I navigated through the water, I was conscious of my right foot's impairments and my decreased ability to avoid stepping on the sharp rocks.

My body's buoyancy in the water assisted me on my journey toward my family on the shore. I realized this unseen but familiar force was lifting me up to make the way easier. It was enabling. It was strengthening. For this, and all the other times I had felt this sublime power, I felt grateful. I decided to embrace this force once again, using my body's buoyancy to its maximum extent by staying low in the water while walking cautiously, step by step, but by my own power, which a loving Heavenly Father had endowed me with.

I came to the shallow waters near the shore. After a brief moment to plan my path to the shore, I stood up—rising—and very deliberately made my way back to my family and back to life.

Years later, looking back at the devastation the stroke had brought, I feel a reverence for the human soul's desire to rise up. While humbly recognizing the unseen assistance we receive, we have the ability to advance our own situation, yet submit to our Father's will, with trust and faith that He has our best interests in the forefront of His majestic mind. Only by realizing our noble potential, as sons and daughters of a God who loves us and desires our growth, can we ascend and rise. Then we can begin to strive and, eventually, achieve our greatest hopes and aspirations. We sometimes realize it's God's love lifting us up. His love is less concrete than that of a kind neighbor rendering service, but His love is as palpable and natural, yet abstract, as gravity. We humans don't really have a way to measure this buoyancy in our lives, but it is there, lifting us up, if we choose to see it.

Eventually, with the passage of time, the gaping holes in my worldview became filled, and my questions were reconciled. Reconciliation, in a spiritual sense, does not mean coming to grips with religion on one's own terms or negotiating with the Lord for the practice of only our favorite parts of the gospel. We don't negotiate the terms of our salvation; we are guided by the Spirit to "seek not to counsel the Lord, but to take counsel from his hand." It is vital for us to have the faith and trust in His "wisdom, and in justice, and in mercy, over all His works. Wherefore, beloved brethren, be reconciled unto Him through the Atonement of Christ, His Only Begotten Son, and ye may obtain a resurrection" (Jacob 4:10-11). It is up to us to seek humbly to align our will with the Father's will, letting Christ steer our ship at times, and wholeheartedly following where He leads us. This does not mean we should "run faster than [we] have strength," but nonetheless, we should be "diligent, that thereby [we] might win the prize" (Mosiah 4:27).

This is necessary, despite, as Apostle Henry B. Eyring explains, "Many of you are now passing through physical, mental, and emotional trials that could cause you to cry out.... One of the keys to an enduring faith is to judge correctly the curing time required."[5] We often need time to sort things out and reconcile their meanings, including trials in our lives, over-extended time—curing time. This also takes humility, which is something not all people possess, but all people can develop. Perhaps, my mortal mind, like most human minds, needed the curing power of time to align my will with the Father's, in humility. The rewards of developing humility can be peace and happiness, of which I can attest.

Eyring further explains, "I cannot promise an end to your adversity in this life.... There are reasons for that.... Those reasons come from this one fact: in Their perfect love for you, our Heavenly Father and the Savior want you fitted to be with Them to live in families forever. Only those washed perfectly clean through the Atonement of Jesus Christ can be there."[6]

It is possible, at some future day, when we look back on our lives, and see the pain and sorrow—the days we had a difficult time just crawling out of bed—we will see the struggle and the joy, and we will rejoice and praise God. Perhaps this is the journey we are destined to take: through trials, exercising faith, reconciliation, and finally, finding peace within our souls. Only now can I see the wisdom of the plan that sets us here on earth to encounter challenges on a road that eventually leads back to the Father.

Love is the reason for the plan—a plan that will reap rewards of eternal happiness. Our Heavenly Father's love for each of us is the reason for the Only Begotten Son, which is Christ, our Lord, to suffer agony in the Garden of Gethsemane to bring about His Atonement. Growth is indeed the purpose of our lives and of mortal existence. Challenges are necessary to facilitate our rising to overcome them, and thereby develop and mature in our ascent. Our Master and Creator has used neurologic principles to create fertile soils in our mortal minds and assist our ascent. His Holy Spirit whispers to our minds, directing us in the path that leads back to Him. Sometimes, this takes the curing power of time. Christ has simplified God's expectations of us by commanding us to love God and love our neighbor. It is our challenge just to put one foot in front of the other…and rise.

Christ's love is available to all. He bears our suffering and gives strength to the weak. He does not cause bad things to happen to people, nor is He responsible for life's misfortunes; rather He is the champion of our ascents in life.

Our Heavenly Father is more wonderful and magnificent than we can presently appreciate. We do not set the stage of our lives, nor can we negotiate their terms. Rather, we can be active players in the intricate drama of mortality, with its twists and turns. With a curious mind, always full of awe, I feel the words of T. S Eliot ring true:

> We shall not cease from exploration.
>
> And the end of all our exploring
>
> Will be to arrive where we began
>
> And to know the place for the first time.[7]

Perhaps, at another time, we will recognize this place because we have passed this way before.

Whether it's facing dramatic loss from a stroke, or whatever this natural, beautiful world throws at us, out of ash, we can triumph. Since the firestorm of my stroke—and because of it—my life has been full of opportunities for growth, redemption, joy, and love, and I am thankful.

I look to the Savior, who created this world and our "imperfectly perfect" bodies, but who also created the tools for us to be receptive to the wonderful world, with opportunities to progress, with unseen assistance, and with whispering guidance. I am growing more and more grateful each day for this time, this space, this life, between His two gardens. Because of things that are difficult and things that are sweet, we can grow. We can feel the love of God. We can give and receive the love of our neighbors, our fellow men and women. And, above all, we can enter into God's love, forever.

A FINAL NOTE

WHERE JUSTICE, LOVE, AND MERCY MEET—BOTH SIDES OF THE TOMB

One of the most troubling events in our collective recent history is one I fear is forgotten in many people's minds: the Rwandan genocide. We seem to take special note of events we deem as the extremes of life. I include this event—my encounter with a survivor of the Rwandan genocide—here because of what it teaches us about the human family and about life on this earth.

I met James at the University Hospital in Salt Lake City in about 2012. He was small, polite, quiet, but articulate—this was odd for a custodial staff member. He was obviously from Africa, and he didn't speak English well. As I learned more about him, a remarkable story began to unfold. James was an immigrant from Rwanda, a Tutsi.

In 1994, I was in a college, a world away from the killings taking place in Rwanda—the largest genocide during my lifetime. I remember hearing the horrific news reports and wondering why someone wasn't doing something. I felt terrible. In the end, powerful nations couldn't or wouldn't do anything to stop the killing. Up to one million people were gruesomely murdered during the 100-day genocide.

James was ten at the time of that genocide. He came from a large and influential family; his dad was a small business owner and his mom a nurse at the local hospital. During those terrible 100 days, his parents and most of his extended family were killed by Hutu neighbors. He survived by hiding deep in the bush for weeks, only moving around at night, and subsisting on natural bushes and occasional bananas from surrounding plantations. He survived because of his boyish yearnings for his mother's love, his hope that she was still alive. The genocide was a nightmare for James and many others like him. Why had God allowed this to happen? It was a question I asked myself upon meeting James.

I am convinced God is intensely interested in how we treat one another, and with how we treat our neighbor. God was not the instigator of this tremendous suffering, but His love was present—for the victims, for the survivors, and even eventually for the perpetrators, as well. In the subsequent years since these killings, numerous stories of reconciliation and even forgiveness of the Hutus by the Tutsis have been told. Most people, when not stirred up by fear and other impulsive emotions, are quite reasonable and loving people. The resiliency and fortitude of the Tutsi survivors is nothing short of a miracle. We can learn numerous lessons in this calamity of the human family from the experience of a whole nation played out in a million separate tragedies.

This topic is one of enormous gravity because, as I am keenly aware, if God's plan of happiness doesn't work for all people, those in faraway places, even those on the fringes, then it doesn't work for any of us. We know life on earth was not set up to be fair. Nothing can be done to bring back James's family, but it is critical to explore and express these events and these emotions. I don't presume to have the answers. Some tragic events require enormous, even extraordinary, faith. I don't suggest I know God's will—His ways and thoughts are higher than mine. But it gives me some comfort to think perhaps God has a much broader view of things like time. Perhaps we should rethink the concept of time, or at least recognize the human limitations of our idea of time. Yet, this I do know: God is intensely interested in the paramount principle of how we treat one another. Christ will make all things right in ways our mortal eyes and minds are just not equipped to see at this time. Nonetheless, questions still remain.

For questions such as why was the Rwandan nation set on turmoil collectively, why did my stroke happen individually—or any senseless bad occurrence—we may be waiting a long, long time for the answers. However, in mortality, if we look with an eye of faith, we see glimpses of God's love shining down on our lives.

When I met James, he was trying to move on with his life and was working hard at two jobs. He was engaged to a young woman named Beatta, also a Tutsi genocide survivor, who still lived in Rwanda. James was trying to wade through the US immigration process to bring her to the United States so they could marry and start a family. I thought about my own ancestor, Joseph Edgley, who emigrated from England with only his one daughter in the 1880s, and worked for many years to get the rest of his family to America. Only through others' generosity was he able to do it. Although different circumstances, the common thread struck a chord with me. James was such a fine man that I envisioned a wonderful future for him and his family if he were able to take that first step. I talked to some contacts and set him up with a wonderful immigration attorney, Elaine Young, who donated her time. I sensed it would take a long time to get the couple reunited in the United States, but time is one of the few things we have, in the space between two gardens. Time may be, in fact, the only thing we can control—at least what we choose to do with our time while we are mortal. What better way to spend time than to foster the potential for love and a new family?

Today, James and Beatta have been married for five years and have a beautiful daughter, with one on the way. With their eyes of faith, they see glimpses of God's love working in their lives. In a life firestorm of this magnitude, often we, as individuals, are called upon to make a choice—a choice whether to allow the firestorm to break us, or to find nourishment among the ashes to create new growth in our lives.

We are all tied to one another, in time and space. Perhaps the opportunity to help James is helping me and others heal our collective guilty conscience about that horrific event all those years ago, when we chose to do nothing. What happened in Rwanda may seem to us like a story in a different time and in a faraway place, but it is a human story, it transcends color or creed—it could have happened to any one of us. Unfortunately, stories similar in solemnity continue to be written and will continue for as long as our human family is subject to being overcome with human emotion and seeing through a glass darkly.

However, there is another reality—the reality of the Savior's Atonement. Seeing that reality requires the faith that transcends the mortal mind and the earthly veil. Jeffrey R. Holland said of the human mind's frailty:

> The simple truth is that we cannot fully comprehend the Atonement and Resurrection of Christ and we will not adequately appreciate the unique purpose of His birth or His death...without understanding that there was an actual Adam and Eve who fell from an actual Eden, with all the consequences that fall carried with it. Because we were then born into that fallen world and because we too would transgress the laws of God, we also were sentenced to the same penalties that Adam and Eve faced. . . every man, woman, and child in it physically tumbling toward permanent death, spiritually plunging toward eternal anguish.[1]

We all need the Atonement of Christ to intercede.

My wife and I had the opportunity to go to Jerusalem, to the Garden of Gethsemane. In this garden, and on the cross, Christ suffered and atoned for my sins, your sins, and the sins of the whole of humankind. After he was crucified, many believe that His body was prepared and placed in what is called the Garden Tomb, a peaceful sanctuary within the Old City. When Emi and I entered what is believed to be that very tomb, we saw a message painted in red on the wall of the tomb: "He is not here; He is risen." The crux of His Atonement is that He has risen, and teaches and enables us also to rise, both in this life and after death. As Emi often points out to me, the Savior's Atonement applies and pertains to both sides of the tomb. In life, it helps us grow and progress, as we struggle, repent, and revise our lives. In this way, His Atonement also aids our development. It helps us rise out of the trials we all experience. In a sense, we all will pass through our personal Garden of Gethsemane, as the poet Ella Wheeler Wilcox explained:

> All paths that have been, or should be
> Pass somewhere through Gethsemane.
> All those who journey, soon or late,
> Must pass within the garden's gate;
> Must kneel alone in darkness there,
> And battle with some fierce despair.
> God pity those who cannot say:
> "Not mine, but thine"; who only pray:
> "Let this cup pass," and cannot see
> The purpose in Gethsemane.[2]

Holland further explains, "from the moment those first parents stepped out of the Garden of Eden, the God and Father of us all...declared to them...that this entire sequence was designed for our eternal happiness. It was part of His divine plan, which provided for a Savior, the very Son of God Himself."[3] The Savior's Atonement would achieve complete victory over physical death, unconditionally granting resurrection to every person who has been born or ever will be born into this world. Furthermore, although terrible things have indeed occurred throughout our human historical past, it takes great faith to comprehend that Christ's Atonement pertains to all of our transgressions and those of others against us. It's no wonder to me that God laid out, in no uncertain terms, the command to love your neighbor, and then sent His most beloved Son to suffer on our behalf. Although not all men know where justice, love, and mercy meet, all who are on this spinning globe will be blessed by His Atonement—eternally.

I recently followed up with a patient, a friend, really, whom I had been seeing for the last seven years. Claire lives near Jackson, Wyoming. She had a stroke at age forty-three. It happened on a Tuesday in late spring as she was running on a trail beside the Snake River where it flows below the foothills of the majestic Teton mountain range near her home. She had been trying to run each day, up and down the mountain canyon trails that had names like Paintbrush Canyon and Cascade Canyon, but running beside the Snake River was her normal route on Tuesdays. She had an idyllic life—married, two kids and living in a place like Eden. As she was running, she noticed a bald eagle circling high above. One can only imagine the scene, in all its splendor and glory, and the way she must have felt, soaking it all in, through her five senses.

Then, without notice, Claire's brain failed to function in the ways she was used to. She began to feel weak in her left leg, then stumbled, and again stumbled, this time falling to the ground. The type of stroke she was having not only made one-half of her body paralyzed, but it also affected the cognition function, making her confused about what was going on and the appropriate next steps in this crisis situation. Not necessarily alarmed by the situation, she was more confused and distracted as she lay on her back looking up at the eagle overhead.

Eventually, a pair of fishermen on a driftboat on the river spotted Claire lying on the trail alongside the river. When they approached her, she was confused, and she calmly asked them to call her husband to pick her up. The fishermen, clearly sensing something was seriously wrong, immediately called 911 and initiated the medical attention she needed. In a sense, she was being expelled from the Garden of Eden to the harsh world of hospitals, treatments, medicine, and doctors in a multi-year effort to regain an element of her previous quality of life.

Today, Claire is fifty-three. She has made the flight from Jackson to the University Medical Center in Salt Lake City dozens of times. She typically comes every three months for treatments and procedures for spasticity, a common condition after stroke when a person's muscles become stiff and hard to move effectively. Over the years, we have become friends; my daughter and her son were born just weeks apart. She loves to travel with her husband and family, and I love hearing of her new adventures. I have always been somewhat surprised because she remained fairly impaired as far as her mobility. Nonetheless, we have always been glad to see each other, even though each time she comes I give her a series of quite painful injections in her spastic muscles.

This last time she visited me after six months (she had missed her regular three-month appointment), she told me that three months ago she had fallen on the ice in Jackson and ruptured her spleen. The spleen had to be removed and the blood loss replaced with a few units of blood through a transfusion, but something unexpected appeared on the routine imaging: a tumor in her abdomen. The tumor was subsequently removed, and found to be a cancerous sarcoma. She is now on an adventure of a different sort—trying to survive a potentially deadly cancer. We both cried in my exam room, lamenting the problems so common to our mortal bodies. I mourned for her; she has been through so much, and, through adaptations, had reached an acceptable quality of life. She says her goal now is to see her grandchildren born, to hold them in her arms. Regardless, I ache for the uncertainty this new diagnosis has brought. The world we live in can be so cruel.

As life goes, historically speaking, it is a relative rarity for God's children to be lucky enough to live into old age. Throughout the ages, the average human life span has been in the thirties or forties or less.[a] Not

[a] A life of eighty-two years equates to 30,000 days, each day filled with struggles, yet joy. We are indeed lucky to have this finite time, to journey, between two gardens. I'm confident we will shout "Hallelujah" when we realize the thousands of tender mercies in all of our lives. All the doubt and pessimism—cast away—and replaced by faith unto endurance, for Christ is our Captain and Hero, who cannot

until the last century have most people lived into their older years. Especially in old age, one has to deal with dozens of "failing parts"; cartilage in the joints wears out and the joints become arthritic, the proteins in the eye's lenses become yellow or cloudy, the soft tissue in vessels like the aorta become calcified, the blood vessels narrow and harden, which in turn produce excess strain on a heart that is already failing to keep up with the demands, and eventually stops working altogether. In every man or woman, systems wear out, and fail, and eventually, the person possessing these organs dies. This is part of Adam's legacy. We are mortal beings. I have to think this is partly what Book of Mormon prophet Moroni meant when he wrote, "And if men come unto me I will show unto them their weakness." Weakness in mortal bodies and mortal minds is what we inherited. But, as Moroni said, by the Father's whisperings of peace, direction, and warnings into our minds, the very minds He created, "weak things become strong" (Ether 12:27).

It is my belief that shortly after we die, we will meet our Lord, Jesus Christ. We will realize that death is normal and the natural order of things—we will all pass through that portal. Normally, a loved one's death is accompanied by great sorrow. This sorrow transcends the mortal realm, but what we don't see as mortals is the homecoming on the other side.

It is hard to imagine the specific details of that homecoming. We only have a few canonized details of it. Personally, I believe that soon after we die, each of us will see and converse with Christ.

I remember fondly the time Emi and I visited the Garden of Gethsemane in Jerusalem, the site of the beginning of the Atonement of Christ—an Atonement that my mortal mind cannot fully grasp or comprehend. I imagine after my death I will meet Christ there, in the Garden of Gethsemane. At that time, all things will be fully grasped. All things will be fully comprehended. All things will be brought to

---

fail. Through His death, we may live and be redeemed, and shall mourn no more.

clear remembrance with the now immortal mind. The weaknesses and mortal frailty, and the primitive synapses in the previous mortal brain will be done away with; the now immortal mind will see clearly and comprehend things we had to take on faith on earth. After all this, even after worms destroy my skin, I imagine myself exclaiming like Job, "yet in my flesh shall I see God" (Job 19:26). Then we will weep… for sorrow, and joy.

We will weep, and remember the growth that came out of hard experience, but we will also see things clearly for the first time, understanding the wisdom and guidance behind all of life's experiences. We will have full comprehension of the Atonement, the information flooding into the now immortal mind, and be able to see sins, regrets, and sorrows. Also, I imagine being able to see the conscious or intentional mind's efforts to follow the two great commandments, and see their shortcomings. Then, we will have full comprehension of the way Christ's Atonement permeates and penetrates every aspect of our lives. Truly, I imagine that, when all things are brought into full recollection and full clarity, the emotions will cause a shout of "Hallelujah!," and we will remember the life that we led. And though it's been said most men live lives of quiet desperation, with no hope except what men mete out by the sweat of their brows, we will yet see. And despite all the unseen biases of men and women, throughout the ages, and the frank evil done by the human mind that is just as inclined to listen to evil voices as good ones, we will yet see with clarity and clairvoyance.

I will shout "Hallelujah!" as I fully realize how the tool we have been given, the mortal mind, even with all its failings, was created by a benevolent God to respond with love to one another. That brain was created to respond to complex and elegant neurotransmitter cascades in a positive way to diverse things…like fields of flowers…or majestic peaks…or art and music, or even to the simple peace of seeing a child peacefully sleeping. I will then see how the creator aligned our brains to respond to the natural world He created and placed us in. Then I will shout "Hallelujah!" With full clarity, I will see the life cycle, with sometimes untimely death, but at other times, with the laying down of the elderly who hath toiled on this earth for a longer time.

Until then, men might think it foolish to believe in this way. But, then again, I don't know another way to believe—a way that is less foolish and more realistic of our experiences of the earth, between two gardens. Author Robert Brault said, "Am I to concern myself with an allotment of days I never had and was never promised? Must I check off each day of my life as if I am subtracting from this imaginary hoard? No, on the contrary, I will add each day of my life to my treasure of days lived. And with each day, my treasure will grow, not diminish."

Through Christ's grace, we can share in His redemption and be enabled and strengthened while living. This grace pertains not just to mortal frailties and death, but to all our mortal travails. We can have peace and hope through sickness and physical challenges, as well as through problems with our families, our employment, depression, anxiety, separation from a loved one, weight problems, body-image difficulties, lack of confidence, or just feeling overwhelmed and not accepting ourselves. We can feel God's love, be redeemed by His love, and be free from the tyranny of mortal trials, and then set our hearts on more fully loving one another, and be free. "Then I find that peace and happiness and love are already given, in plain view, in the ongoing work of caring for the world."[4]

The Atonement of Jesus Christ, says Jeffrey R. Holland, enables us to partake in the "gift of victory over every fall we have ever experienced, every sorrow we have ever known, every discouragement we have ever had, every fear we have ever faced,"[5] and on the other side of the tomb, the biggest and most complete victory of all—triumph over death. Through the afflictions of man—stroke, cancer, death—and the evils we sometimes inflict on our neighbor, truly, we can be of good cheer. Even though in this world we will all have tribulation, we will be able to shout "Hallelujah" because Christ has overcome the world (John 16:33).

Because of the limited human minds and imperfect bodies we possess, we do not fully comprehend our Heavenly Father's perfect plan. C. S. Lewis insightfully wrote, "That is what mortals misunderstand. They say of some temporal suffering, 'No future bliss can make up for it,' not knowing that Heaven, once attained, will work backwards and turn even that agony into a glory.... And that is why, at the end of all things, when the sun rises here...the blessed will say, 'We have never lived anywhere except in Heaven.'"[6]

"We have the promise of a blessed future that inspires and upholds us through the bends and bumps in life's journey," explains Dieter F. Uchtdorf. Furthermore, "As you accept His sacrifice, become His disciple, and finally reach the end of your earthly journey, what will become of the sorrows you have endured in this life? They will be gone. The disappointments, betrayals, persecution you have faced...gone. The suffering, heartache, guilt, shame, and anguish you have passed through—gone...forgotten."[7]

It's up to each one of us to believe in the prophets and apostles' words—to believe we can change, to do the hard work we were meant to do, to trust in the Savior to steer our ship. We know this life and these experiences with these mortal bodies are designed to give us the experiences we need in order to return to Him, our Heavenly Father. We can have faith in that process, over and over, every day of our life.

For LOVE *always* wins. CHRIST *is* the victory story.

END NOTES

Chapter 1: Two Gardens

1 Dew, Sheri. *If Life Were Easy, It Wouldn't Be Hard.* Salt Lake City, UT: Deseret Book Company, 2005. p. 6.
2 Zimmerman, Anthony. *Evolution and the Sin in Eden.* New York: UP of America, 1998. p. 152-53.
3 Holland, Jeffrey R. *Christ and the New Covenant.* Salt Lake City, UT: Deseret Book Company, 1997. p. 238.
4 Bednar, David A. "The Atonement and the Journey of Mortality." *Ensign.* (May 2012).
5 Ibid.
6 Nelson, Russell M. *The Gateway We Call Death.* Salt Lake City, UT: Deseret Book Company, 1995. p. 3.

Chapter 2: Preparing for the Firestorm

1. Dew, Sheri. *If Life Were Easy, It Wouldn't Be Hard.* Salt Lake City, UT: Deseret Book Company, 2005. p. 8.
2. Maxwell, Neal A. "My Servant Joseph." *Ensign.* (April 1992).
3. Edgley, Richard C. "Three Towels and a 25-Cent Newspaper." *Ensign.* (Nov 2006).
4. Christofferson, D. Todd. "Building Faith in Christ." *Ensign.* (Sept 2012).

Chapter 3: Silent Before God

1. Gombrich, E. *A Little History of the World.* New Haven, CT: Yale UP, 1985. p. 187.
2. Bono, Edward de. *Six Thinking Hats.* New York: Little Brown, 1985. p. 52.
3. Ibid. p. 34.
4. Kushner, Harold. *When Bad Things Happen to Good People.* New York: Schocken Books, 1981. p. 60.

Chapter 4: Exploring Christ, the Healer

1. Holland, Jeffrey R. "Songs Sung and Unsung." *Ensign*. (May 2017).
2. Renlund, Dale G. "Our Good Shepherd." *Ensign*. (May 2017).
3. Givens, Fiona and Terryl Givens. *The Christ Who Heals*. Salt Lake City, UT: Deseret Book Company, 2017. p. 64.
4. Ibid, p. 65.
5. Oaks, Dallin H. "Healing the Sick." *Ensign*. (May 2010).
6. Givens, Fiona and Terryl Givens. *The Christ Who Heals*. Salt Lake City, UT: Deseret Book Company, 2017. p. 77.
7. Lynberg, Michael. *Make Each Day Your Masterpiece*. Kansas City, KS: Andrews McMeel, 2001. p. 7.
8. Frost, Robert. "Stopping by Woods on a Snowy Evening." *In The Poetry of Robert Frost: Stopping by Woods on a Snowy Evening*. New York: Holt, Rinehart, and Winton, 1969.
9. Oliver, Mary. *Winter Hours: Prose, Prose Poems, and Poems*. Boston, MA: Houghton Mifflin Company, 1999. p. 31.
10. Miller, Adam S. *An Early Resurrection*. Salt Lake City, UT: Deseret Book Company, 2018, p. 7.
11. Ibid. p. 9.

Chapter 5: Doing the Hard Things

1. Kennedy, John F. *Good Reads*. Retrieved July 31, 2018 from Quotable Quotes: https://www.goodreads.com/quotes/493205-we-choose-to-go-to-the-moon-in-this-decade
2. Bush, George W. "A Day of Terror: Bush's Remarks to the Nation on the Terrorist Attacks." September 12, 2001. Retrieved from *New York Times*: https://www.nytimes.com/2001/09/12/us/a-day-of-terror-bush-s-remarks-to-the-nation-on-the-terrorist-attacks.html
3. Bednar, David A. "Ye Must Be Born Again." *Ensign*. (May 2007).
4. Kimball, Spencer W. "The False Gods We Worship." *Ensign*. (June 1976).
5. Nelson, Russell M. *The Gateway We Call Death*. Salt Lake City, UT: Deseret Book Company, 1995. p. vii.

6. Quindlen, Anna. *A Short Guide to a Happy Life*. New York: Random House, 2000, p. 25-26.
7. Bednar, David A. "That We Might "Not...Shrink."" *CES Devotional for Young Adults*. Arlington, TX, 2013.
8. Maxwell, Neal A. "Applying the Atoning Blood of Christ." *Ensign*. (Nov 1997).

Chapter 6: Choosing Faith and Seeing Tender Mercies

1. Anderson, Neil L. "You Know Enough." *Ensign*. (Nov 2008).
2. Pew Research Center. *The Global Religious Landscape*. December 18, 2012. Retrieved from PewForum.org: www.perforum.org/2012/12/18/global-religious-landscape-exec/.
3. Holland, Jeffrey R. "Lord, I Believe." *Ensign*. (May 2013).
4. Olsen, Andrew. *The Price We Paid*. Salt Lake City, UT: Deseret Book Company, 2006, p. 1-3.
5. Givens, Terryl and Fiona Givens. *The God Who Weeps*. Salt Lake City, UT: Ensign Peak, 2012. p. 4.
6. Hugo, Victor. *Les Misérables*. 1862. Trans. Charles Wilbour. New York: Fawcett Premier, 1961, p. 121.
7. Ibid. p. 457.
8. Miller, Adam S. *An Early Resurrection*. Salt Lake City, UT: Deseret Book Company, 2018, p. 85.
9. Kipling, Rudyard. *Kipling Society Homepage*. Retrieved February 22, 2018 from http://kipling.org.uk/kip_fra.htm.

Chapter 7: When a Door Closes, Make a New One

1. Lewis, C. S. *Mere Christianity*. New York: MacMillan, 1980, p. 176.
2. Oaks, Dallin H. "Strengthened by the Atonement of Jesus Christ." *Ensign*. (Nov 2015).
3. Ibid.
4. Givens, Fiona and Terryl Givens. *The Christ Who Heals*. Salt Lake City, UT: Deseret Book Company, 2017. p. 1.

Chapter 8: Stand, Act, and Endure to the End

1. Boy Scouts of America. filestore.scouting.org. Retrieved August 12, 2018 from Wilderness Survival Merit Badge Series: https://filestore.scouting.org/filestore/merit_badge_regandres/wilderness_survival.pdf
2. Groberg, John H. *The Other Side of Heaven*. Salt Lake City, UT: Deseret Book Company, 1993. p. 5.
3. Meshberger, Frank L. "An Interpretation of Michelangelo's Creation of Adam Based on Neuroanatomy." *JAMA* (1990): 1837-41.
4. Sabin, Gary B. "Stand Up Inside and Be All In." *Ensign*. (May 2017).
5. Broderick, Carlfred. (2008). *The Uses of Adversity*. Salt Lake City, UT: Deseret Book Company, 2008. p. 7.
6. Milton, John. *Paradise Lost*. 1667. Malden, MA: Blackwell, 2007.

Chapter 9: The Human Capacity for Happiness: A Neurological and Spiritual Perspective

1. Thoreau, Henry David. *Walden, or, Life in the Woods*. 1854. New York: E.P. Dutton, 1908.
2. Ibid.
3. Davidson, Richard. *The Emotional Life of Your Brain*. New York: Plume, 2012. p. 104.
4. Davidson, Richard. "The Science of a Happy Mind, Part 1." *National Geographic*. Feb 2018. Retrieved from https://video.nationalgeographic.com/video/ng-live/160321-davidson-healthy-mind-part1-lecture-nglive
5. Weng, Helen Y. et al. "Compassion Training Alters Altruism and Neural Responses to Suffering." *Psychological Science*. (2013). p. 1171-1180.
6. Lynberg, Michael. *Make Each Day Your Masterpiece*. Kansas City, KS: Andrews McMeel, 2001, p. 106.
7. Gilbert, Daniel. *Stumbling on Happiness*. New York: Vintage Books, 2007.
8. Givens, Terryl and Fiona Givens. *The God Who Weeps*. Salt Lake City, UT: Ensign Peak, 2012. p. 33-34.

9. Lynberg, Michael. *Make Each Day Your Masterpiece*. Kansas City, KS: Andrews McMeel, 2001. p. 14.
10. Keats, John. "Do You Not Think." *In The Letters of John Keats*. London, Gr. Brit.: Reeves & Turner, 1895.
11. Davidson, Richard. "The Science of a Happy Mind, Part 1." *National Geographic*. Feb 2018. Retrieved from https://video.nationalgeographic.com/video/ng-live/160321-davidson-healthy-mind-part1-lecture-nglive
12. Benson, Ezra T. "Born of God." *Ensign*. (July 1989).
13. Lynberg, Michael. *Make Each Day Your Masterpiece*. Kansas City, KS: Andrews McMeel, 2001. p. 96.
14. Weng, Helen Y. et al. "Compassion Training Alters Altruism and Neural Responses to Suffering." *Psychological Science*. (2013) p. 1171-1180.

Chapter 10: The Scars of Bethesda

1. McGrath, Collicutt. "Post-traumatic growth in acquired brain injury: A preliminary small scale study." *Brain Injury*. (2006): 767-773.
2. Tedeschi, R. G. et al. *The Handbook of Posttraumatic Growth: Research and Practice*. New York: Psychology Press, 2014.
3. McGrath, Collicutt. "Post-traumatic growth in acquired brain injury: A preliminary small scale study." *Brain Injury*. (2006): 767-773.
4. Tyson, J. "Turning a tragedy into a tribute: A literature review of creating meaning after loss of a loved one." *Illness, Crisis, & Loss*. (2013): 325-340.
5. Tedeschi, R. G. et al. *The Handbook of Posttraumatic Growth: Research and Practice*. New York: Psychology Press, 2014.
6. McGrath, Collicutt. "Post-traumatic growth in acquired brain injury: A preliminary small scale study." Brain Injury. (2006): 767-773.
7. Waldinder, Robert. "Becoming Wise." *TED Radio Hour*. Aired June 10, 2016. www.npr.org/programs/ted-radio-hour/481290551/becoming-wise.
8. Salter, Katherine. *Community Reintegration*. September 10, 2008. Retrieved from The Evidence-Based Review of Stroke Rehabilitation: www.ebrsr.com.

9. Whitman, Walt. "Manly Health and Training, with Off-Hand Hints Toward Their Conditions." *Walt Whitman Quarterly Review*. 33 (2016).
10. Tedeschi, R. G. et al. *Posttraumatic Growth: Conceptual Foundation and Empirical Evidence*. Philadelphia: Lawrence Erlbaum Associates, 2004.
11. Thoreau, Henry David. Retrieved February 20, 2018 from http://www.goodreads.com/quotes/803686-happiness-is-like-a-butterfly-the-more-you chase-it.
12. Teresa, Mother. Retrieved February 20, 2018 from https://www.goodreads.com/quotes/33359-let-no-one-ever-come-to-you-without-leaving-better.
13. Tedeschi, R. G. et al. *The Handbook of Posttraumatic Growth: Research and Practice*. New York: Psychology Press, 2014.
14. Miller, Adam S. *An Early Resurrection*. Salt Lake City, UT: Deseret Book Company, 2018, p. 66.
15. Givens, Fiona and Terryl Givens. *The Christ Who Heals*. Salt Lake City, UT: Deseret Book Company, 2017, p. 84-85.
16. Ulrich, Wendy. *The Temple Experience*. Springville, UT: Cedar Fort, 2012, p. 8-9.
17. Kalanithi, Paul. *When Breath Becomes Air*. New York: Random House, 2016, p. 98.

Chapter 11: Relationships, Good Intentions, and Consequences in Our Natural World

1. Hinckley, Gordon B. "Be Not Faithless." *Ensign*. (May 1978).
2. Montgomery, James. "A Poor Wayfaring Man of Grief." *Hymns of the Church of Jesus Christ of Latter Day Saints*. Salt Lake City, UT: Deseret Book Company, 1985. p. 29.

Chapter 12: Hearts Knit Together in Unity with Our Neighbor

1. Oaks, Dallin H. "Bible Stories and Personal Protection." *Ensign*. (Nov 1992).
2. Kotlowitz, Alex. *There Are No Children Here*. New York: Doubleday, 1991.

3. Homes, Henry Horner. *Wikipedia/Henry Homer Homes.* Retrieved August 19, 2018 from Wikipedia: www.en.m.wikipedia.org/wiki/henry_horner-homes.
4. Givens, Terryl and Fiona Givens. *The Crucible of Doubt.* Salt Lake City, UT: Deseret Book Company, 2014, p. 47.
5. Ibid. p. 46-47.
6. Hemingway, Ernest. *A Farewell to Arms.* New York: Scribner, 1929.

Chapter 13: Love Is the Reason for Our Travails Between Two Gardens

1. Uchtdorf, Dieter F. "The Love of God." *Ensign.* (Nov 2009).
2. Ibid.
3. Ibid.
4. Kimball, Spencer W. "Give Me This Mountain." *Ensign.* (Nov 1979).
5. Eyring, Henry B. "Mountains to Climb." *Ensign.* (May 2012).
6. Ibid.
7. Eliot, T. S. "Little Gidding." Retrieved January 14, 2019 from http://www.columbia.edu/itc/history/winter/w3206/edit/tseliotlittlegidding.html.

A Final Note: Where Justice, Love, and Mercy Meet—Both Sides of the Tomb

1. Holland, Jeffrey R. "Where Justice, Love, and Mercy Meet." *Ensign.* (May 2015).
2. Wilcox, Ella W. "Gethsemane." *The Courier-Journal.* (Aug 1887).
3. Holland, Jeffrey R. "Where Justice, Love, and Mercy Meet." *Ensign.* (May 2015).
4. Miller, Adam S. *An Early Resurrection.* Salt Lake City, UT: Deseret Book Company, 2018. p.117.
5. Holland, Jeffrey R. "Where Justice, Love, and Mercy Meet." *Ensign.* (May 2015).
6. Lewis, C. S. *The Great Divorce.* San Francisco: Harper, 1946.
7. Uchtdorf, Dieter F. "Behold the Man!" *Ensign.* (May 2018).

BIBLIOGRAPHY

Anderson, Neil. L. "You Know Enough." *Ensign*. (Nov 2008).

Ballard, M. Russell. "Suicide." *Ensign*. (Oct 1987).

Ballard, M. Russell. *Our Search for Happiness*. Salt Lake City, UT: Dereset Book Company, 1993.

Bible, King James Version. Salt Lake City, UT: The Church of Jesus Christ of Latter-day Saints, 1977.

Bednar, David A. "Ye Must Be Born Again." *Ensign*. (May 2007).

Bednar, David A. "The Atonement and the Journey of Mortality." *Ensign*. (May 2012).

Bednar, David A. "That We Might "Not...Shrink"." *CES Devotional for Young Adults*. Arlington, TX, 2013.

Benson, Ezra T. "Born of God." *Ensign*. (July 1989).

Bono, Edward de. *Six Thinking Hats*. New York: Little Brown, 1985.

Book of Mormon. Salt Lake City, UT: The Church of Jesus Christ of Latter-day Saints, 1989.

Boy Scouts of America. *filestore.scouting.org*. Retrieved August 12, 2018 from Wilderness Survival Merit Badge Series: https://filestore.scouting.org/filestore/merit_badge_regandres/wilderness_survival.pdf

Broderick, Carlfred. (2008). *The Uses of Adversity*. Salt Lake City, UT: Dereset Book Company, 2008.

Bush, George W. "A Day of Terror: Bush's Remarks to the Nation on the Terrorist Attacks." September 12, 2001. Retrieved from *New York Times*: https://www.nytimes.com/2001/09/12/us/a-day-of-terror-bush-s-remarks-to-the-nation-on-the-terrorist-attacks.html

Christofferson, D. Todd. "Building Faith in Christ." *Ensign*. (Sept 2012).

Davidson, Richard. *The Emotional Life of Your Brain*. New York: Plume, 2012.

Davidson, Richard. "The Science of a Happy Mind, Part 1." *National Geographic*. Feb 2018. Retrieved from https://video.nationalgeographic.com/video/ng-live/160321-davidson-healthy-mind-part1-lecture-nglive

Dew, Sheri. *If Life Were Easy, It Wouln't Be Hard*. Salt Lake City, UT: Deseret Book Company, 2005.

Dew, Sheri. *Worth the Wrestle*. Salt Lake City, UT: Dereset Book Company, 2017.

Doctrine and Covenants. Salt Lake City, UT: The Church of Jesus Christ of Latter-day Saints, 1989.

Edgley, Richard C. "Three Towels and a 25-Cent Newpaper." *Ensign*. (Nov 2006).

Eliot, T. S. "Little Gidding." Retrieved January 14, 2019 from http://www.columbia.edu/itc/history/winter/w3206/edit/tseliotlittlegidding.html.

Eyring, Henry B. "Mountains to Climb." *Ensign*. (May 2012).

Faust, James E. "The Healing Power of Forgiveness." *Ensign*. (May 2007).

Frost, Robert. "Stopping by Woods on a Snowy Evening." In *The Poetry of Robert Frost: Stopping by Wood on a Snowy Evening.* New York: Holt, Rinehart, and Winton, 1969.

Gilbert, Daniel. *Stumbling on Happiness.* New York: Vintage Books, 2007.

Givens, Fiona and Terryl Givens. *The Christ Who Heals.* Salt Lake City, UT: Dereset Book Company, 2017.

Givens, Terryl and Fiona Givens. *The God Who Weeps.* Salt Lake City, UT: Ensign Peak, 2012.

Givens, Terryl and Fiona Givens. *The Crucible of Doubt.* Salt Lake City, UT: Dereset Book Company, 2014.

Gleerup, Craig. *The Type of Marriage that Endures.* Mustang, OK: Tate Publishing & Enterprises, 2007.

Gombrich, E. *A Little History of the World.* New Haven, CT: Yale UP, 1985.

Groberg, John H. *The Other Side of Heaven.* Salt Lake City, UT: Deseret Book Company, 1993.

Hafen, Bruce C. *A Disciple's Life: The Biography of Neal A. Maxwell.* Salt Lake City, UT: Dereset Book Company, 2002.

Hemingway, Ernest. *A Farewell to Arms.* New York: Scribner, 1929.

Hinckley, Gordon B. "Be Not Faithless." *Ensign.* (May 1978).

Hinckley, Gordon B. *Standing for Something.* Salt Lake City, UT: Deseret Book Company, 2000.

Hoffman, Roger. "Consider the Lilies of the Field." Bountiful, UT: Jackman Music Corporation, n.d.

Holland, Jeffrey R. *Christ and the New Covenant.* Salt Lake City, UT: Deseret Book Company, 1997.

Holland, Jeffrey R. "Lord, I Believe." *Ensign*. (May 2013).

Holland, Jeffrey R. "Where Justice, Love, and Mercy Meet." *Ensign*. (May 2015).

Holland, Jeffrey R. "Songs Sung and Unsung." *Ensign*. (May 2017).

Homes, Henry Horner. *Wikipedia/Henry Homer Homes*. Retrieved August 19, 2018 from Wikipedia: www.en.m.wikipedia.org/wiki/henry_horner-homes.

Hudson, H. Director. *Chariots of Fire*. 1981. With Ben Cross and Ian Charleson.

Hugo, Victor. *Les Misérables*. 1862. Trans. Charles Wilbour. New York: Fawcett Premier, 1961.

Kalanithi, Paul. *When Breath Becomes Air*. New York: Random House, 2016.

Keats, John. "Do You Not Think." In *The Letters of John Keats*. London, Gr. Brit.: Reeves & Turner, 1895.

Kennedy, John F. *Good Reads*. Retrieved July 31, 2018 from Quotable Quotes: https://www.goodreads.com/quotes/493205-we-choose-to-go-to-the-moon-in-this-decade

Kimball, Spencer W. "The False Gods We Worship." *Ensign*. (June 1976).

Kimball, Spencer W. "Give Me This Mountain." *Ensign*. (Nov 1979).

Kipling, Rudyard. *Kipling Society Homepage*. Retrieved February 22, 2018 from http://kipling.org.uk/kip_fra.htm.

Kotlowitz, Alex. *There Are No Children Here*. New York: Doubleday, 1991.

Kushner, Harold. *When Bad Things Happen to Good People*. New York: Schocken Books, 1981.

Lewis, C. S. *The Great Divorce.* San Francisco: Harper, 1946.

Lewis, C. S. *Mere Christianity.* New York: MacMillan, 1952.

Lynberg, Michael. *Make Each Day Your Masterpiece.* Kansas City, KS: Andrews McMeel, 2001.

Maxwell, Neal A. "According to the Desire of [Our] Hearts." *Ensign.* (Nov 1996).

Maxwell, Neal A. "Applying the Atoning Blood of Christ." *Ensign.* (Nov 1997).

Maxwell, Neal A. "My Servant Joseph." *Ensign.* (April 1992)

McGrath, Collicutt. "Post-traumatic growth in acquired brain injury: A preliminary small scale study." *Brain Injury.* (2006): 767-773.

Meshberger, Frank L. "An Interpretation of Michelangelo's Creation of Adam Based on Neuroanatomy." *JAMA* (1990): 1837-41.

Miller, Adam S. *An Early Resurrection.* Salt Lake City, UT: Deseret Book Company, 2018.

Milton, John. *Paradise Lost.* 1667. Malden, MA: Blackwell, 2007.

Montgomery, James. "A Poor Wayfaring Man of Grief." *Hymns of the Church of Jesus Christ of Latter Day Saints.* Salt Lake City, UT: Deseret Book Company, 1985. p. 29.

Mormon Doctrine. Salt Lake City, UT: Bookcraft, 1966.

Muhlestein, Kerry. *Why We Must Be Wholeheartedly Holy.* Retrieved May 12, 2015 from https://speeches.byu.edu/talks/kerry-m-muhlestein_why-we-must-be-wholeheartedly-holy.

Nelson, Russell M. *The Gateway We Call Death.* Salt Lake City, UT: Deseret Book Company, 1995.

Nelson, Russell M. "Ministering." *Ensign*. (May 2018).

Oaks, Dallin H. "Bible Stories and Personal Protection." *Ensign*. (Nov 1992).

Oaks, Dallin H. "Healing the Sick." *Ensign*. (May 2010).

Oaks, Dallin H. "Strengthened by the Atonement of Jesus Christ." *Ensign*. (Nov 2015).

Oliver, Mary. *Winter Hours: Prose, Prose Poems, and Poems*. Boston, MA: Houghon Mifflin Company, 1999.

Olsen, Andrew. *The Price We Paid*. Salt Lake City, UT: Deseret Book Company, 2006.

Pew Research Center. *The Global Religious Landscape*. December 18, 2012. Retrieved from PewForum.org: www.perforum.org/2012/12/18/global-rerligious-landscape-exec/.

Quindlen, Anna. *A Short Guide to a Happy Life*. New York: Random House, 2000.

Renlund, Dale G. "Our Good Shepherd." *Ensign*. (May 2017).

Sabin, Gary B. "Stand Up Inside and Be All In." *Ensign*. (May 2017).

Salter, Katherine. *Community Reintegration*. September 10, 2008. Retrieved from The Evidence-Based Review of Stroke Rehabilitation: www.ebrsr.com.

Shakespeare, William. *Goodreads.com*. Retrieved February 2018 from https://www.goodreads.com/quotes/56164-what-win-i-if-i-gain-the-thing-i-seek.

Simon, Sidney B. and Suzanne Simon. *Forgiveness: How to Make Peace with Your Past and Get On with Your Life*. New York: Warner Books, 1990.

Smith, J. *History of the Church of Jesus Christ of Latter Day Saints, Vol. 5*. Ed. B. H. Roberts. Salt Lake City, UT: Deseret Book Company, 1957.

Teachings of the Presidents of the Church: Spencer W. Kimball. Salt Lake City, UT: The Church of Jesus Christ of Latter Day Saints, 2006.

Tedeschi, R. G. et al. *The Handbook of Posttraumatic Growth: Research and Practice*. New York: Psychology Press, 2014.

Tedeschi, R. G. et al. *Posttraumatic Growth: Conceptual Foundation and Empirical Evidence*. Philadelphia: Lawrence Erlbaum Associates, 2004.

Teresa, Mother. Retrieved February 20, 2018 from https://www.goodreads.com/quotes/33359-let-no-one-ever-come-to-you-without-leaving-better.

Thoreau, Henry David. *Walden, or, Life in the Woods*. 1854. New York: E.P. Dutton, 1908.

Thoreau, Henry David. Retrieved February 20, 2018 from http://www.goodreads.com/quotes/803686-happiness-is-like-a-butterfly-the-more-you chase-it.

Tyson, J. "Turning a tragedy into a tribute: A literature review of creating meaning after loss of a loved one." *Illness, Crisis, & Loss*. (2013): 325-340.

Uchtdorf, Dieter F. "A Yearning for Home." *Ensign*. (Nov 2017).

Uchtdorf, Dieter F. "The Love of God." *Ensign*. (Nov 2009).

Uchtdorf, Dieter F. "The Merciful Obtain Mercy." *Ensign*. (May 2012).

Uchtdorf, Dieter F. "Behold the Man!" *Ensign*. (May 2018).

Ulrich, Wendy. *The Temple Experience*. Springville, UT: Cedar Fort, 2012.

Waldinder, Robert. "Becoming Wise." *TED Radio Hour*. Aired June 10, 2016. www.npr.org/programs/ted-radio-hour/481290551/becoming-wise.

Weng, Helen Y. et al. "Compassion Training Alters Altruism and Neural Responses to Suffering." *Psychological Science*. (2013).

Whitman, Walt. "Manly Health and Training, with Off-Hand Hints Toward Their Conditions." *Walt Whitman Quarterly Review*. 33 (2016).

Wilcox, Ella W. "Gethsemane." *The Courier-Journal*. (Aug 1887).

Zimmerman, Anthony. *Evolution and the Sin in Eden*. New York: UP of America, 1998.

ABOUT THE AUTHOR

STEVEN EDGLEY is an Associate Professor in the Division of Physical Medicine & Rehabilitation and is the Director of Stroke Rehabilitation at the University of Utah. He survived a massive stroke at the age of twenty-eight. He is involved with both the clinical aspects of stroke rehabilitation and with research on new techniques and methods to promote, facilitate, and improve life after stroke. His aim is to help patients through clinical care and practical applications to achieve greater independence and quality of life after a stroke.

Dr. Edgley graduated from Brigham Young University in 1997, with medical school completion at Loyola University in Chicago in 2001. He completed his residency in Physical Medicine and Rehabilitation in 2006 at the University of Utah in Salt Lake City, Utah, and received his board certification with the American Board of Physical Medicine and Rehabilitation in 2007. In 2013, Dr. Edgley was given the Healthcare Hero Award by *Utah Business Magazine* for his advocacy of stroke patients, which is inspired by his personal experience. He and his wife Emi live in Salt Lake City, Utah, and are the parents of two daughters, Ella and Louisa. In his free time, he enjoys hiking, skiing, waterskiing, and cycling.